fashioned for INTIMACY

JANE HANSEN AND MARIE POWERS

Gospel Light

AGLOW.
INTERNATIONAL

Gospel Light is an evangelical Christian publisher dedicated to serving the local church. We believe God's vision for Gospel Light is to provide church leaders with biblical, user-friendly materials that will help them evangelize, disciple and minister to children, youth and families.

We hope this Gospel Light resource will help you discover biblical truth for your own life and help you minister to adults. God bless you in your work.

For a free catalog of resources from Gospel Light please contact your Christian supplier or call 1-800-4-GOSPEL.

PUBLISHING STAFF
William T. Greig, Publisher
Dr. Elmer L. Towns, Senior Consulting Publisher
Dr. Gary S. Greig, Senior Consulting Editor
Jill Honodel, Editor
Pam Weston, Assistant Editor
Kyle Duncan, Associate Publisher
Bayard Taylor, M.Div., Editor, Theological and Biblical Issues
Barbara LaVan Fisher, Cover Designer
Debi Thayer, Designer

ISBN 0-8307-2321-8
© 1998 Jane Hansen and Marie Powers
All rights reserved.
Printed in U.S.A.

Aglow International is an interdenominational organization of Christian women. Our mission is to lead women to Jesus Christ and provide opportunity for Christian women to grow in their faith and minister to others.

Our publications are used to help women find a personal relationship with Jesus Christ, to enhance growth in their Christian experience, and to help them recognize their roles and relationships according to Scripture.

For more information about our organization, please write to Aglow International, P.O. Box 1749, Edmonds, WA 98020-1749, U.S.A., or call (425) 775-7282. For ordering or information about the Aglow studies, call (800) 793-8126.

CONTENTS

PREFACE

When the apostle Paul poured out his heart in letters to the young churches in Asia, he was responding to his apostolic call to shepherd those tender flocks. They needed encouragement in their new lives in Jesus. They needed solid doctrine. They needed truth from someone who had an intimate relationship with God and with them.

Did Paul know as he was writing that these simple letters would form the bulk of the New Testament? We can be confident that the Holy Spirit did! How like God to use Paul's relationship with these churches to cement His plan and purpose in their lives and, generations later, in ours.

We in Aglow can relate to Paul's desire to bond those young churches together in the faith. After 1967, when Aglow fellowships began bubbling up across the United States and in other countries, they needed encouragement. They needed to know the fullness of who they were in Christ. They needed relationship. Like Paul, our desire to reach out and nurture from far away birthed a series of Bible studies that have fed thousands since 1973 when our first study, *Genesis*, was published. Our studies share heart-to-heart, giving Christians new insights about themselves and their relationships with and in God.

God's generous nature has recently provided us a rewarding new relationship with Gospel Light Publications. Together we are publishing our Aglow classics, as well as a selection of exciting new studies. Gospel Light began as a publishing ministry much in the same way Aglow began publishing Bible studies. Henrietta Mears, one of its visionary founders, formed Gospel Light in response to requests from churches across America for the Sunday School materials she had written for the First Presbyterian Church in Hollywood, California. Gospel Light remains a strong ministry-minded witness for the gospel around the world.

Our hearts' desire is that these studies will continue to kindle the minds of women and men, touch their hearts and refresh spirits with the light and life a loving Savior abundantly supplies.

This study, *Fashioned for Intimacy*, explores God's original design for the relationships between men and women, then moves into a discovery of His plan for reconciliation between men and women and Himself. I know its contents will reward you richly.

Jane Hansen
International President
Aglow International

INTRODUCTION

Jesus, Whom heaven must receive [and retain] until the time for the
complete restoration of all that God spoke.
Acts 3:20,21 (*AMP*)

Many things are being restored in our day. Perhaps most significant is the restoration of
relationships in the Body of Christ. Sweeping movements of reconciliation are covering the
land. God is moving by His Spirit today to reconcile races, cultures and denominations.

In *Fashioned for Intimacy*, we address the final front: the healing of the rupture within
each race, within each culture, within each denomination—the division between male and
female, not only in individual couples but in the corporate Church as well.

The Holy Spirit is restoring our vision, opening our eyes as never before to see areas of
prejudice, places we have hurt and wounded one another in every level of relationship. God
is answering Jesus' final prayer for His Church, "that they all may be one…that the world
may believe that You [Father] sent Me" (John 17:21). The Holy Spirit is preparing the family of God for the return of Christ!

Although our introductory Scripture verse indicates that all things will be restored prior
to Jesus' release from heaven to return to earth, it does not mean that the earth and all the
ills of the world will be restored and somehow miraculously made right. Isaiah 60:2 states
that "darkness shall cover the earth, and deep darkness the people." Yet God brackets these
words of foreboding with a marvelous prophecy to His people that will be happening at the
same time. "Arise, shine;" God tells His people, "For your light has come! And the glory of
the LORD is risen upon you….the LORD will arise over you, and His glory will be seen upon
you" (vv. 1,2). This is what we see Him doing today; He is restoring His house, His dwelling
place, that He might come and fill it with His glory.

From the beginning, He made known His intent: "So God created man[kind] in His own
image;…male and female….Then God blessed them…and said to them…'fill the earth and

subdue it [and] have dominion...over [it]'" (Genesis 1:27,28). Thus was announced the beginning place, the foundation of the House of the Lord—the place where He would dwell. Male and female, man and woman, the fundamental union specifically fashioned by God to vividly and accurately display His image, His heart, His character in the earth.

God's plan was not a secret. It had been publicly declared to the universe and God's archenemy had heard it. The enemy knew that the plan's success depended on the unity and trust of these two people, for together they bore God's image.

Once again Satan endeavored to rise up against God, to exalt his throne, his rule, above the throne of God, and he knew right where to strike (see Isaiah 14:13,14). He knew it was essential to bring separation, distrust, fear and suspicion between male and female, the image bearers God purposed to use for His unfolding plan on earth. The strength of man and woman was in their union. Without unity, without oneness, God's plan would fail.

Satan struck and his strategy worked. In shame, blame and distrust Adam and Eve covered themselves from each other even before they hid from God. God's original design was broken, His image corrupted.

We know that the human race continues to suffer the fallout from Satan's malignant coup, but the sad truth is that the Church itself has not fully recovered from this catastrophic event. We in the Body of Christ have yet to experience a very key and vital reconciliation—that between man and woman—and as a result the work of God suffers great loss. This relationship, above all others, is the foundational place from which God will work to accomplish His ultimate intention.

In *The Fashioned for Intimacy Study Guide* we explore what was truly in the heart of God as He brought forth that first man and woman and the factors that continue to militate against the fulfillment of all that He purposed to accomplish in and through their lives.

AN OVERVIEW OF THE STUDY

The chapters in this Bible study are divided into four sections:

- A CLOSER LOOK AT THE PROBLEM defines the problem and the goal of the study.
- A CLOSER LOOK AT GOD'S TRUTH gets you into God's Word. What does God have to say about the problem? How can you begin to apply God's Word as you work through each lesson?
- A CLOSER LOOK AT MY OWN HEART will help you clarify and further apply truth. It will also give guidance as you work toward change.
- ACTION STEPS I CAN TAKE TODAY is designed to help you concentrate on immediate steps of action.

As you work through this study guide, you will gain greater understanding of...

- What God's original design for His Church is.
- How Satan's strike at the heart of God's design—male and female—continues to weaken and cripple marriage, family, the Church and society to this day.

- How this crippling is lived out in our relationships with God and with each other so that we are robbed of the intimacy God intended to satisfy both His heart and ours.
- Biblical truths that will again restore us to God's original design and empower us to fulfill our mandate of purpose in the earth.

This study guide can be used for personal Bible study, small groups, Sunday School classes or as a group leader's guide.

You Will Need

1. A Bible.
2. A copy of *Fashioned for Intimacy*; the book is used as a text and is referenced in every chapter by page numbers.
3. A notebook in which to write your answers to the questions.
4. A copy of the study guide. In group study, a copy of the Bible study guide for each participant, while not a necessity, would provide them with a record of the questions asked and increase clarity of understanding.
5. Time to meditate on what you're learning.

GROUP LEADERS

This study guide has been designed to make leading a group a manageable task for anyone willing to do so. The study guide follows the book chapter by chapter. Each chapter of the study guide contains commentary that summarizes the main emphases of the book followed by questions and Scripture studies to further explore the main points. The commentary will be of great assistance and will provide ease and cohesiveness as you move the participants through the questions.

Answers to most questions are referenced to the book as well as further Scripture study but all questions are meant to challenge, stimulate and draw out the thinking of the participants. Many of the questions will stimulate discussion that will more than fill the allotted time for most classes. If you desire to cover a chapter per week in your group, you may want to set time limits on the discussions in order to get through all the material given.

For Optimal Benefit

1. Each person should come to the group having read at least the chapter of the book to be studied in the current session. In a large group there may be those who have come unprepared. They will still profit from the study.
2. As group leader, it will be important to have completed the appropriate chapter study before each class so that you are familiar with the content and prepared for the discussion.

HOW TO START AND LEAD A SMALL GROUP

———— ❧❧❧ ————

One key to starting and leading a small group is to ask yourself, What would Jesus do and how would he do it? Jesus began His earthly ministry with a small group of disciples. The fact of His presence made wherever He was a safe place to be. Think of a small group as a safe place. It is a place that reflects God's heart, God's hands. The way in which Jesus lived and worked with His disciples is a basic small group model that we are able to draw both from direction and nurture.

Paul exhorts us to "walk in love, as Christ also has loved us and given Himself for us" (Ephesians 5:2). We, as His earthly reflections, are privileged to walk in His footsteps, to help bind up the brokenhearted as He did or simply to listen with a compassionate heart. Whether you use this book as a Bible study, or as a focus point for a support group, a church or home group, walking in love means that we "bear one another's burdens" (Galatians 6:2). The loving atmosphere provided by a small group can nourish, sustain and lift us up as nothing else does.

Jesus walked in love and spoke from an honest heart. In His endless well of compassion He never misplaced truth. Rather, he surrounded it with mercy. Those who left His presence felt good about themselves because Jesus used truth to point them in the right direction for their lives. When He spoke about the sinful woman who washed Jesus' feet with her tears and wiped them with her hair, He did not deny her sin. He said, "her sins, which are many, are forgiven, for she loved much" (Luke 7:47). That's honesty without condemnation.

Jesus was a model of servant leadership. "Whoever desires to become great among you shall be your servant. And whoever of you desires to be first shall be slave of all" (Mark 10:43,44). One of the key skills a group leader possesses is to be able to encourage the group members to grow spiritually. Keeping in personal contact with each member of the group, especially if one is absent, tells each one that he/she is important to the group. Other skills an effective group leader will develop are: being a good listener, guiding the discussion, and guiding the group to deal with any conflicts that arise within it.

Whether you're a veteran or brand new to small group leadership, virtually every group you lead will be different in personality and dynamics. The constant is the presence of Jesus Christ, and when He is at the group's center, everything else can come together.

9

YOU'RE INVITED!

———◦◦◦———

To grow...

To develop and reach maturity; thrive; to spring up; come into existence from a source;

with a group

An assemblage of persons gathered or located together; a number of individuals considered together because of similarities;

To explore...

To investigate systematically; examine; search into or range over for the purpose of discovery;

new topics

Subjects of discussion or conversation.

Meeting on

Date _____ Time_____

Located at

Place _____

_____

Contact _____

Phone _____

One

THE FATHER AND HIS FAMILY

He also has planted eternity in men's hearts and minds [a
divinely implanted sense of a purpose working through the
ages which nothing under the sun but God alone can satisfy].
Ecclesiastes 3:11 (*AMP*)

There is in each of us, whether Christian or not, a sense that life must have a purpose, that it must consist of more than mere survival skills—that it must be made up of more than climbing to the top of the ladder of success and the accumulation of money and goods to prove our worth and existence. Ecclesiastes 3:11 tells us that this sense of purpose comes from God. It also declares that only God Himself can satisfy it. Only God can reveal to our hearts what our purpose is and only God can satisfy our deep longings for significance.

God's plan and purpose for us is very carefully designed. He did not leave us to guess at what it is. Our goal in this chapter is to begin our discovery of God's very clear design, what motivated His design and what has threatened it from the beginning of time.

A Closer Look at the Problem

1. Read the falcon story and the comments under the subheading "Reflecting on the Falcons" (on pages 17-19). To what does Jane attribute the fascination of an entire city with a mere bird family?

The central theme in God's plan for humanity on the earth was the concept of family. There is something innate within us that responds to family, even a bird family, because the Creator of the universe has marked our hearts with the need for love, belonging, unity, warmth and safety. All of these are the dynamics of a family as God designed it to be.

Never before in history has the family been so violently under siege. Not only are families falling apart at unprecedented rates, but the very concept of family as we have known it is being attacked as outmoded, declared by many to no longer be of any practical value. Some are declaring that the conventional concept of family is hostile and discriminatory and they have attempted to redefine "family." "When the backbone of God's framework crumbles, all of life is thrown out of joint. Pain, disintegration, dysfunction and brokenness will be the excruciating result" (p. 24).

2. Describe some of the pain and dysfunction that society is suffering because God's framework—the family—is suffering such great assault.

3. Describe ways that some people attempt to replace family when they leave their own biological family.

What are they looking for?

The Church is not exempt from this onslaught of family breakdown. The difference in the divorce rate within the Church and without is negligible. Even a family that appears to be intact does not guarantee that love and caring are the dynamic of the home.

The "house of God" in Scripture is a term for the "household" or "family" of God—the Church. First Peter 4:17 declares that "the time has come for judgment to begin at the house of God."

First Corinthians 11:32 in the *Amplified* version reads: "But when we [fall short and] are judged by the Lord, we are disciplined and chastened, so that we may not [finally] be condemned [to eternal punishment along] with the world."

4. What do you think moves the heart of God to judge His own people (see Hebrews 12:5,6)?

A Closer Look at God's Truth

"FATHER," A RELATIONAL TERM

5. Do you tend to view the term "father" as biological or relational? What constitutes one as a father?

In our broken society today, we can easily forget that the word "father" is intended to be inherently relational. It identifies a type of relationship *to* someone.

Describe what you think would be most significant to a loving father's heart. Would it be merely the number of children he would have or would there be something more in his desire for a family? What would that be?

Does this affect your viewpoint of God? Explain how.

6. The book of Ephesians is the revelation of God's plan and purpose for His family [the Church] from before the foundation of the world. Read Ephesians 1:3-6. What does Ephesians 1:3-6 tell us was God's design for us from before the foundation of the world?

Note: "Sons" (Greek, *huios*) in Scripture, when referring to God's people, is inclusive of male and female. "Sons" is an important term that denotes those who are heirs and who are moving toward maturity through the nurture, training and discipline of the Holy Spirit. Such training is to prepare the sons—heirs—for the "receiving [of the] kingdom" (Hebrews 12:28) "prepared for [us] from the foundation of the world" (Matthew 25:34). See Romans 8:14-17; Galatians 3:26—4:7; Hebrews 12 and Revelation 21:7. "Sons" is a term that denotes a full inheritance.

7. Read Hebrews 2:9,10. Describe how God has made every provision for His plan and purpose for us to come to complete fulfillment.

What does this tell us about the heart of God for His children?

FAMILY—AN OUTFLOW OF THE FATHER'S HEART

God's most basic, fundamental nature is that of a Father. All of His creative work issued out of His Father-heart's desire for a family. Initially, He created a home for His future children. When it was ready, He created the first members of His family, fashioned in His own image, to dwell in it. Adam and Eve were then given the privilege of enlarging God's family as well as stewardship over the earth as God commanded them to "Be fruitful and multiply; fill the earth and subdue it; have dominion over...the earth" (Genesis 1:28).

8. Read Ephesians 3:14,15 in several translations. From whom does this passage tell us that the family derives its name—nature, character, design? (Note: "Name" in Scripture denotes "honor, authority, character."[1])

Which family is our earthly family intended to represent?

Why do you think God gave us this experiential example?

THE FAMILY LINE

9. On pages 22-24 we speak of "the family line." What action of God was His crowning endorsement of family?

    Read Luke 2:51,52. What are we told happened to Jesus within the framework of family?

    What does this say about God's confidence in His creation of family?

    Does this fact affect your viewpoint of family? How?

THE FOUNDATION OF THE FAMILY

The foundation of something is the beginning place. To verify the foundation of family we have to go to the beginning.

10. According to Genesis 1:27,28, who is the beginning or the foundation of the family?

    This family was not just "a family." Whose family were they?

    Who are the beginning or the foundation of God's family, house or household?

11. The Church is the New Testament name for the family, house or household of God. Based on your answers to question 10, who is the foundation of the Church? (We are not referring here to the theological truth of Jesus and the apostles. We are speaking of the practical functioning of the Church.)

ONLY GOD CAN SET THINGS RIGHT

12. On pages 25-26, Pastor McIntosh is quoted as saying, "So often we hear that the world is too intense, too violent, too ugly, and that is what is destroying our homes. It is not the world that is destroying our homes. It is the weakness of our homes that is destroying our world." Respond to Pastor McIntosh's comments. Do you agree? Why?

Pastor McIntosh is right. The health of society depends on the health of families. The health of families, however, depends on the health of the parents—how they function together as male and female.

Male and female are the initial foundation of everything God has planned to do. Working together as God designed, they are the strength of society, family and the Church. One does not have to puzzle long to discover the roots of the problem of our fragmenting world. The failure lies with us—whether male or female—we are part of the problem.

God's plan to have a family in His likeness who would represent Him on the earth was spoken out clearly at the beginning of time. "Satan heard, and launched his attack at the heart of the plan" (p. 26).

13. Who was the very heart of God's plan and thus the target of Satan's attack?

14. Read Psalm 133. In this psalm what are we told is the basis for God's blessing on a people?

If there is disunity, what can we conclude will be the result?

Read Matthew 18:18,19; 1 Peter 3:7 and Malachi 2:13-16. Respond to these scriptures in light of Psalm 133.

15. In a word, what is the most critical quality of all relationships, beginning with male and female?

    Therefore, what can we expect Satan to be constantly doing and what are some ways we can see his activity played out?

A Closer Look at My Own Heart

God wants to heal the rupture in His Church. We have begun to see the Spirit moving to bring greatly needed reconciliation on two important fronts—racially and denominationally.

Now, He is bringing us further. He wants to heal the division within each race and within each denomination—the division between male and female, the foundation of His house. Not only does He want to heal individual couples, but the alienation and separation of male and female in the Church as well.

God's design is a family for Himself, together forming a house in which He desires to dwell and express Himself in love and in power throughout the earth.

16. Think of and record ways you are living your life consistently or inconsistently (or both) with the fact that you are part of God's larger family created for His pleasure and purpose.

17. As you consider how essential unity and relationships are to the fulfillment of His plan, can you think of attitudes or behaviors in your life that need to be reevaluated? If so, what are they?

Action Steps I Can Take Today

18. Write out Psalm 133 and place it where you can see it often this week.

19. Pray and ask God to reveal to you areas where you may have prejudices or attitudes that affect the way you relate to some of the Body of Christ, God's family. Pay special attention to male/female areas. If any come to mind, ask someone to pray with you for freedom. Remember, based on 1 John 1:7, if God reveals any wrong attitudes to you He will be faithful to bring you to wholeness in these areas.

Note:
1. James Strong, *Strong's Exhaustive Concordance* (Grand Rapids, Mich.: Baker Book House, 1984), #8034, p. 117.

- Two -

ESTORATION

For the time being [Jesus] must remain out of sight in heaven
until everything is restored to order again just the way God,
through the preaching of his holy prophets of old, said it
would be. Acts 3:21 (*The Message*)

In chapter 1 we noted that God's plan for His family is very clearly stated in
Scripture. Yet we see the Church far from His intended design. We are not discouraged, however. Our confidence is based on the very nature of God Himself—He is a God of restoration.

First Peter 4:19 calls God a "faithful Creator." This means that God did not
just create humanity and then leave us to flounder and struggle to find our
own way. He would be faithful to bring us to His desired destination if we
would but trust Him. When Paul declared that he was "confident of this very
thing, that He who has begun a good work in you will complete it until the day

of Jesus Christ" (Philippians 1:6), he was not speaking of a new expression of God's love that began with the advent of Jesus Christ. He was revealing the character and nature of God as it has always been—faithful to His creation. God would complete and fulfill what He had started. The coming of Christ was the ultimate evidence of God's faithfulness. "Jesus, the Creator of the universe, died to restore that which He created" (p. 32).

Our goal in this chapter is to establish in our hearts God's faithfulness to restore that which He created and to begin to discover precisely what He is determined to restore. We have slightly revised the order of subheadings in this chapter for the sake of continuity of study.

A Closer Look at the Problem

Today we see little resemblance to the wonderful and perfect world God created at the beginning of time. Because of the Fall, nature and humanity have suffered a death blow and we see the results all around us. The pristine beauty of nature as God designed it is now constantly at war with itself. Weeds, thorns, thistles, drought, disease and insects threaten to choke out God's beauty at every turn. It is a never-ending battle to keep gardens and fields free of these encroaching enemies in order to preserve some semblance of what we instinctively know is God's design for our world.

Humanity, too, is at war with itself. The lust, greed and covetousness that are at the root of the world's moral decay (see 2 Peter 1:4, *AMP*) are the predators that daily threaten to choke out the very life of the human race. Like the carpet in Jane's bedroom, our hearts have become stained and marred, needing to be replaced with new ones (see p. 30).

1. Read Jeremiah 13:23; 17:9,10. What do these verses tell us about humanity's condition before God and our ability to help ourselves?

2. Read Ezekiel 36:25-27. What is our only answer?

A Closer Look at God's Truth

GOD'S HEART

"Restoration is not just something on the heart of God; it is the heart of God!...Restoration is the reason Jesus came to earth" (p. 31).

3. Read John 1:29; Hebrews 4:3 and Revelation 13:8b (last phrase, in translations other than *NASB*). In view of these three passages, when was our deliverance accomplished?

   How does Christ's death for us demonstrate the nature of God as a "faithful Creator" (1 Peter 4:19)?

4. Jesus died not only to redeem us from the Fall but also to restore us to God's original intention for us. Write down Webster's definition for "restore" given at the top of page 32.

"God's purpose in sending Jesus was that we would receive restoration in every dimension of our lives: body, soul, spirit and purpose" (p. 32).

5. Read Isaiah 53:4,5 and Ephesians 2:5,6. Explain how these verses affirm the above statement and Webster's definition of "restore."

GOD'S REPRESENTATIVE

Although the full restoration of our bodies will not come until eternity, God's intention is that restoration of spirit, soul and purpose should begin in this lifetime.

6. Read Genesis 1:26-28. In this passage we learn two things about God's design for humankind: what they would be like and what they were to do. What are we told they would be like?

Although both aspects of God's design for humanity were extremely important, which do you think would be of first importance to God: what we are like or what we do? Why?

7. Recall the meaning of the word "image" (see p. 35). What does this key word tell us was God's plan and purpose for His family?

God wants to restore us to His image and likeness. In order for this to happen we have to know what His image and likeness is. Jesus came to earth to demonstrate the nature of God as "the exact likeness of the unseen God" (Colossians 1:15, *AMP*), so that in beholding Him we could know the Father, what He is like, and be changed into His image (see 2 Corinthians 3:18).

Yet long before this happened, God wanted His people to know Him. A beautiful and poignant example of this is in Exodus 34:6,7 where God personally tells Moses what He is like in His own words. In response to Moses' request to know Him (see Exodus 33:13,18) God declares that He will show Moses His glory by showing him His goodness (vv. 19-23).

8. Read Exodus 34:6,7 (correlate v. 7 with Exodus 20:5,6). Write down the character qualities that God declares about Himself.

9. Read Galatians 5:22,23 which describes the fruit of the Spirit. Note the similarities with the list God gives concerning Himself. What, then, is the purpose of the work of the Spirit in us?

CORPORATE HEADQUARTERS

"God's plan for redemption and restoration is not only individual, but it is also corporate" (p. 32). Matthew 5:18 in the *Amplified* version reads:

> For truly I tell you, until the sky and earth pass away and perish, not one smallest letter nor one little hook...will pass from the Law until all things [it foreshadows] are accomplished.

10. Read Matthew 22:36-40 and Romans 13:8. What are we told is the fulfillment of the law?

Jesus came to do this—to fulfill the law. What single event in His life demonstrated both Jesus' total love for the Father and His immeasurable love for humanity at the same time (see John 14:28-31; 15:13)?

11. Read Romans 8:3,4. What do these verses tell us Jesus came to do in us?

Jane declares: "When Scripture states that the heavens will retain Him until all things have been restored, it is telling us that Jesus will not return for a Body that is still divided, weak and broken, a Body of people who blindly walk in darkness, oblivious to God's plan and purpose for them" (p. 32). The intent of the law was always to establish and maintain a people in right relationship with God (see Exodus 20:1-11) and with each other (see vv. 12-17). The law, however, could only govern their outward behavior.

12. Referring to the above statement, what is the main focus of God's restoring work?

Read the opening Scripture verse again. Notice that this verse is not referring to the whole world. It is referring to God's plan and purpose for His people.

13. When everything is restored to order in the Church and the law is fulfilled in us, how will the world know and what will they know? Why (see John 13:34,35; 17:23)?

AN UNPRECEDENTED MOVE—ALL MEANS ALL
"Restoration has begun!" (p. 33).

One of the unique activities of God in the past 30 years has been an unmistakable move by His Spirit on the hearts of women in never-before-seen numbers. We will go into much more detail concerning this phenomenon in later chapters and how it specifically relates to God's present work of restoration. For the moment, however, let's consider just one aspect of the significance of this action on God's part.

14.   Read Ephesians 1:11,12. What things do these verses tell us God works according to the counsel of His will and what is the end result of His working?

Without discussing further details at this time, what can we know about this unprecedented move of God among women based on the above verses of Scripture?

RESTORATION OF PURPOSE

"God's purpose in sending Jesus was that we would receive restoration in every dimension of our lives: body, soul, spirit and purpose" (p. 32).

Earlier we asked the question, "Which do you think would be of first importance to God—what we are like or what we do?" The answer is, "What we are like." We can only do what we have been created to do when our actions flow out of who we are as we're changed into God's likeness through the renewing of the Holy Spirit in our hearts. Yet God has designed us for purpose: "For we are His workmanship, created in Christ Jesus for good works, which God prepared beforehand that we should walk in them" (Ephesians 2:10).

15.   Genesis 1:28 describes what God created humanity to do. Read the verse, then write it down.

16.   Review the meanings of the words "fruitful" and "multiply" on page 36. From these definitions what do you see as a larger meaning than just increasing in numbers? Explain.

17.   Review the meaning and comments concerning the word "subdue" found on the same page. Explain what this word means.

18.   Reread the definition of *kabash* (subdue) quoted on page 36. According to this definition and since plants and animals were in harmony with humans before the Fall, who would be the most likely force that would need to be subdued?

19. According to the "law of first mention" (see p. 36), what do the words "increase," "multiply," "subdue" and "dominion" tell us about Adam and Eve's purpose?

This was a daunting task for the first couple, far too much for mere humans to accomplish. Satan, after all, "had been 'the anointed cherub who covers,' indicating high office and having authority and responsibility to protect and defend the holy mountain of God" (p. 37). There was a gaping inequality of power and experience between Satan and these two inaugural humans.

20. Read 2 Corinthians 4:7 and 12:9. What clue do these verses give us that may explain God's actions? (We will explore this further in subsequent chapters.)

A Closer Look at My Own Heart

21. Write down your thoughts and/or share them with your group as you consider the following questions:

As you contemplate the very nature of God's heart as a restoring God and His commitment to you as a "faithful Creator," are there areas in your life or circumstances that you have felt were beyond God's ability to restore?

Or do you feel that it's too late, that even though you are a Christian, you have ignored God's call to His complete Lordship too long and He no longer has a significant purpose for you?

Perhaps there are loved ones in your life who have gone so far from God that you fear God may just wash His hands of them and no longer pursue them.

How does the truth in this chapter affect your viewpoint?

Action Steps I Can Take Today

God wants to restore us to His image and likeness. In order for this to happen we have to personally know Him. We can be born again and still not really know the Father's heart. The main focus of God's desire is to restore us to relationship, first of all with Himself. As we come to know Him, we become more like Him—conformed to His image. Restoration to right relationship with ourselves, others and restoration of purpose will flow out from there.

22. Read God's promise to you in Hebrews 8:8-12. These are God's words, His commitment to you. All who desire to know Him shall know Him. He delights to respond to you just as He did to Moses. He will tell you and demonstrate to your heart who He is, what He is like. This is His covenant to you which flows out of who He is—a restoring God who is in love with His children!

    a. Is there anything holding you back from taking God at His Word in your life? If so, ask your heavenly Father to remove these obstacles and make a commitment to allow Him to take away anything that blocks you from fully receiving His promises to you.

    b. As you pray, remind yourself and God what you are grateful to Him for.

Three

A TALE OF TWO TREES

The tree of life was also in the midst of the garden, and the
tree of the knowledge of good and evil. Genesis 2:9

From before the foundation of the earth God had a mandate of purpose for His offspring, of which Adam and Eve were the beginning. They came into the world with work to do, a work of great magnitude. They were to "be fruitful and multiply; fill the earth and subdue it; have dominion over the fish of the sea, over the birds of the air, and over every living thing that moves on the earth" (Genesis 1:28).

Adam and Eve were created in the image and likeness of God. That is, they were created with the capacity to be like God and represent Him in the earth as His stewards according to God's design and purpose. They were to fill the earth with the image and glory of God as they reproduced children who would also be in God's likeness.

We noted in our last chapter that Adam and Eve came into the world with an existing opponent who also wanted control of God's creation—a hostile adversary who would use all of his splendor and cunning wisdom to prevent them from accomplishing their task. This hostile force was Satan, the one who had challenged God in the heavenlies and would now challenge Him through His first created children on earth. Part of Adam and Eve's training for "sonship" (attaining maturity and coming into their full inheritance) included learning to subdue and overcome this powerful adversary. This unbalanced situation—mere humans pitted again the most beautiful and powerful being ever created—"was to be the 'schoolroom' of their learning" (p. 39).

The goal of this chapter is to discover and emphasize:

a.   The essential need for the life of God within the believer and the fact that this plan did not originate with the coming of Christ but was God's design from the inception of His plan for a family. Everything God wanted to do in and through humanity hinged on the consummation of this event.

b.   The dangerous condition Adam was in as he ignored God's provision for him.

A Closer Look at the Problem

Let's review, for a few moments, some of the qualities of Satan—whom they were to tread underfoot—so we can see just what Adam and Eve were up against.

1.   Read Ezekiel 28:11-19. The *Spirit-Filled Life Bible* says of these verses: "Vv. 14,15 are the most conclusive evidence that this text likely refers to Satan's fall."[1] Write down some of the king of Tyre's qualities, remembering that we are looking at the king of Tyre as a personification, or type, of Satan. Let the splendor and magnificence of this being sink into your consciousness. (At the top of page 37 in chapter 2, we describe the meaning of some of the terms used in this passage.)

2.   Describe the kind of being it would take to subdue this amazing creature.

$\mathcal{A}$ $\mathcal{C}$loser $\mathcal{L}$ook at $\mathcal{G}$od's $\mathcal{T}$ruth

It would require beings of incredible power and wisdom to deal effectively with Satan. They would have to have superhuman, supernatural ability. In reality, only God Himself was wiser and more powerful than this creature who was "the seal of perfection, full of wisdom and perfect in beauty" (v. 12). Let's discover the solution for Adam and Eve who were so outclassed by their enemy.

GOD'S PROVISION

3. Read Genesis 2:9,16,17. What were the two main trees in the Garden of Eden?

4. Read John 6:35,53-58. From these verses, what can we infer that the tree of life represents (also see pp. 43-45)?

5. Describe the significance of the tree of the knowledge of good and evil (see p. 44).

6. In regard to the trees mentioned in Genesis 2:9,16,17, what was Adam commanded to do first (also see Nee's quote, p. 43)?

7. Write down the literal translation of the first part of Genesis 2:16 found at the bottom of page 44.

   Why was the first part of the command so important?

8. Read Galatians 5:16, Ephesians 6:10,11 and James 4:7. Describe how these verses confirm the order of God's command to Adam in Genesis 2:9,16,17.

Jesus is the pattern Man, the "second Man" (1 Corinthians 15:47), who came to fulfill what the "first man" failed to do.

9. Quickly review the story of the beginning of Jesus' ministry in Luke 3:21-23; 4:1-19. What event immediately precedes the statement in verse 23: "Now Jesus Himself began His ministry at about thirty years of age"?

Discuss or write down the significance of this order in Jesus' life, especially as it relates to His temptation in the wilderness where He is directly confronted by Satan and also as it relates to His ministry to the sick and the bound.

10. Read John 5:19,30; 14:10. By whose life did Jesus live?

We see that Jesus, even though He had been conceived by the Holy Spirit, needed a second impartation of the Spirit of God to begin and to fulfill His ministry. We see this pattern in the lives of the first disciples as well.

11. Read John 20:22—which was spoken to the disciples by Jesus after He rose from the dead—and Acts 1:4,8. How do these two passages affirm the pattern of two impartations?

The disciples had received the Holy Spirit when Jesus breathed on them before His ascension, but it was after they obediently waited for and received the second impartation as the Spirit was poured forth from heaven that they became empowered to represent Him—be His witnesses—in the earth. They would do the works that Jesus did, "and greater works" would they do through the empowerment of the Holy Spirit (see John 14:10-18).

The same is true for Adam. Even though Adam had become a living soul when God breathed on him as recorded in Genesis 2:7, he needed more to fulfill the calling of God on his life. As DeVern Fromke declared, "Perhaps nothing has so blighted the vision and growth of believers as the false assumption that Adam in his innocence and sinlessness was all that God ever purposed him to be" (p. 44).

God's provision for Adam was a further impartation of His own life, represented by the tree of life, of which Adam must partake voluntarily. So essential was Adam's choice to eat that "his life depended on it. The future of God's plan depended on it. Authority over the enemy depended on it" (p. 43).

12. Read Genesis 3:22. What does this verse tell us would have happened to Adam if he had partaken of the tree of life even after he had sinned?

Since Adam would have lived forever had he partaken of the tree of life after he had sinned, what would have happened to him if he had partaken of it before he sinned?

Did Adam live forever?

What can we conclude was Adam's response to the tree of life? Did he ever eat of it?

The life that God was offering Adam was eternal life which overcomes all things. It would have provided him with everything he needed for "life and godliness" (2 Peter 1:3). It could not be snuffed out by death. We can deduce from Genesis 3:22 that Adam never partook of this life.

13. Since Adam was not partaking of the tree of life as his source of life, what life was he depending on?

In the beginning, Adam's neglect of the tree of life did not appear to be an evil thing, but the activity of the flesh—life that issues from the self-center—does not always immediately appear evil.

14. Review Nee's comments on the self on page 49 and the description of self which follows. As human beings we have three main enemies: the world, the flesh (self) and the devil. Which of these three is the most dangerous? Why?

15. Read James 1:14,15. How does verse 14 affirm the truth that self is our greatest enemy?

16. Romans 5:19, *Amplified*, reads: "For just as by one man's disobedience (failing to hear, heedlessness, and carelessness) the many were constituted sinners." What does this verse tell us about Adam?

17. "Carelessness in attitude is the precursor (forerunner) of actual disobedience."[2] What was Adam being careless about before he actually sinned?

ALONE IS NOT GOOD

Adam's position was precarious. He was on the brink of disaster. The story of the prodigal son and the father's heart describes for us the depth of love in the heart of the heavenly Father for His first created son. Knowing the catastrophic results if Adam chose to go his own way, He would do everything He could to help him before it was too late.

To fully appreciate Adam's situation, we must consider the words that are used as God speaks of him. Immediately after Adam is commanded in Genesis 2:16,17 to eat abundantly and freely of all the trees provided for his sustenance, inclusive of the tree of life and exclusive of the tree of the knowledge of good and evil, God declares, "It is not good that the man should be alone; I will make him an help meet [suitable] for him" (v. 18, *KJV*). "Alone" is the key word here. Literally it means "separation."

18. Review and write down Genesis 2:18 from Berry's *The Interlinear Literal Translation of the Hebrew Old Testament* found on page 50.

At this point only God and the animals were present in Adam's life. Review the passage on page 43 taken from Watchman Nee's book *The Messenger of the Cross*. Even though Adam has not sinned at this point, he is not advancing as he should. He is yet separated. From whom and why?

19. Discuss as a group or write your answer to the following: What would be the difference between the terms "alone" and "lonely" (as some have inferred from Genesis 2:18)?

Only God is greater than Satan. Only through God's life in us can we subdue Satan. Only God's life in us can subdue us (see Micah 7:19; Romans 5:10). Only God's life in us can "overcome the world" (John 16:33). "Christ [Messiah, the Savior, the very life of God!] in you, the hope of glory" (Colossians 1:27) has ever and always been God's provision and plan for His children. God's own life in us and upon us has always been the intended culmination of everything He has done. But this life must be voluntarily received, then cultivated.

20. Read Luke 9:23,24. What did Jesus mean by this statement?

Dependence on our own life and strength must be seen as futile and renounced, turned from, denied. In this chapter we have seen how critical this truth was for Adam. He, too, was required to deny his own life, even though it was not yet marred by sin, and to be abundantly filled with the life of God in order to fulfill his calling. We saw that Jesus followed this pattern. Though sinless, He denied His own life and lived wholly by the life of the Father.

A Closer Look at My Own Heart

Even though we have been justified—"just-as-if-I'd-never-sinned," restoring us to a condition similar to that of Adam before the Fall—and born again, we can still be living our life out of our own strength.

21. Considering the truths we have studied in this chapter…

Can you say that you have left your self-dependence behind?

Do you still, for the most part, live your life by the tree of the knowledge of good and evil, i.e., do you govern your life by setting up standards or rules you have established by determining what is good and what is evil, thereby trying to do good and please God in your own strength?

Or have you learned how to partake of Jesus through His Word, have fellowship with the Father and be changed from the inside so that the life of the Spirit is the spontaneous result of your fellowship?

Think about these things and write down your thoughts as you discuss them with your group.

Action Steps I Can Take Today

22. Take your thoughts before the Father in Jesus' name. Tell Him that you know He created you to have fellowship with Him and represent Him in the earth and that you can only do this by His life in you. Ask Him to give you discernment and a greater revelation of how to live by His life and not your own.

23. If you are not sure that you have received the full provision of God through the baptism of the Holy Spirit, ask someone to pray with you for this essential blessing and equipping by the Father. He will be faithful to answer these prayers for "this is the confidence that we have in Him, that if we ask anything according to His will, He hears us. And if we know that He hears us, whatever we ask, we know that we have the petitions that we have asked of Him" (1 John 5:14,15).

24. Find someone who understands the truth of "walking by the Spirit," living by the life of Christ within, who can encourage you and strengthen you in your quest.

Notes:

1. Jack Hayford, Editor, *Spirit-Filled Life Bible* (Nashville, Tenn.: Thomas Nelson Publishers, 1991), p. 1195. Verse 13 would also lend credence to this view. The king of Tyre could not have been in the Garden of Eden because in his time it no longer existed.
2. W.E. Vine, *An Expository Dictionary of New Testament Words* (Grand Rapids: Fleming H. Revell Co., 1966), p. 319.

- *Four* -

SHE SHALL BE CALLED WOMAN

Then the rib which the LORD God had taken from man He
made into a woman, and He brought her to the man.
Genesis 2:22

As we begin this chapter there is a problem in paradise. Until this time God
had pronounced as "good" all of His works. Now, for the first time, we hear
God saying something is not good. "It is not good that man should be alone"
(Genesis 2:18). A solution is needed. That solution, in God's creative wisdom,
would be woman.

The goal of this chapter is to illuminate the bringing forth of the woman. We
want to discover what her purpose is. When we know her purpose, we will
then begin to understand who she is and what she will be like because God
designed her specifically in answer to what He was observing.

A Closer Look at the Problem

In the previous chapter we left Adam in a precarious condition. God had commanded him to eat abundantly and freely of the trees in the garden, most particularly the tree of life which represented the provision of God's life for Adam. Adam must partake of this tree volitionally (by his own choice and action). The fruit of the tree of life was absolutely essential to Adam. Without it he would be "vulnerable to the voice of the enemy, weak in resisting the desires of his own flesh and eventually [his neglect] would lead him to overt sin and rebellion against ...God" (p. 48). Adam, however, was ignoring God's provision. He was being careless and heedless toward God's positive command (p. 48).

1. Read Genesis 2:16-18. To what situation is God speaking when He declares, "It is not good that the man should be alone; I will make him an help meet [suitable] for him" (v. 18, *KJV*)?

2. In the second account of the creation found in Genesis 2, the first mention of the woman is in verse 18. Notice that she is introduced to us by the word "help." For what will the woman be designed to be a help?

   What did we learn is the meaning of the word "alone" (see p. 50)?

A Closer Look at God's Truth

HIS OTHER SELF

In this section we learn something profound about the identity of the woman. Genesis 2:21,22 tells us that "[God] took one of [Adam's] ribs, and closed up the flesh in its place. Then the rib which the LORD God had taken from man He made into a woman, and He brought her to the man."

3. These verses are the only time the Hebrew word *sela* is translated as "rib." Review the larger meaning of *sela* at the top of page 52. Write down the statement quoted from the *Theological Wordbook of the Old Testament*.

Respond to this statement as a group or write down some of your own thoughts as you meditate upon it.

4. Read Genesis 2:23. Adam recognized Eve as "bone of my bones and flesh of my flesh." Who was he saying she was?

    Review Ephesians 5:28,33 from Vincent's *Word Studies in the New Testament* found on page 56. What are these verses telling us?

5. Read Genesis 1:27. Describe the two-step process of the creation of man (see p. 53).

6. The first part of Genesis 1:27 tells us that "God created man in His own image." When the woman was taken out of the man, what happened to the image of God?

    If the image of God was divided when the woman was differentiated out of the man, how is the image of God made full again?

7. The taking of Adam's bride out of his side was a foreshadowing of another event that was to come. What was it (see page 52)?

    What does this tell us about God's value and perspective on marriage?

LEAVE AND CLEAVE

When the woman was brought forth, "something of Adam's own self was removed from him and returned to him in a very different package" (p. 52). No sooner had God performed His divine surgery, however, than He immediately gave Adam an instruction.

Right after Adam delightfully declared, "This is now bone of my bones and flesh of my flesh; she shall be called Woman because she was taken out of

Man" (Genesis 2:23), God responded. Because Adam recognized who the woman was—part of his own self—God gave him a directive that was a statement about how He intended Adam to relate to this gift.

8. Read verse 24, remembering that it is directly following Adam's statement. What does "Therefore" refer to and why is the man to cleave to his wife?

   What does verse 24 tell us will happen when the man cleaves to his wife? What did they begin as?

   Who is told to do the cleaving (*KJV*) (notwithstanding the vows in many marriage ceremonies)?

9. When the woman was taken out of the man, he was no longer the same as before. Part of him was missing. What happens to him when he cleaves to his wife?

   Pursue this idea further. What characteristics, qualities, etc. does a man receive back to himself when he cleaves to his wife? Write down your ideas.

10. The Hebrew word for "cleave" is *dabaq* which means "to cling, stick to, follow closely, or join to." Was this cleaving to be merely a sexual joining or was there a deeper meaning to the instruction? What did God have in mind?

HELP IN TIME OF TROUBLE

Before the woman is called woman in the account of creation in Genesis 2, she is called a "help." According to the "law of first mention"—the first place something is mentioned in Scripture, which sets the groundwork for all further references to that same subject—we need to let the meaning of this word settle into our spirits.

11. Review and write down the meaning of "help" (*ezer* in Hebrew) from the bottom of page 56. Include the explanation of its contextual usage.

What does this word tell us about Adam's condition?

What does this word tell us about the seriousness of the gift God was giving the man?

"'Help' or *ezer* is an extremely strong word, used 21 times in Scripture. Sixteen times it refers to divine help (God Himself), five times to human help" (p. 56).

12. "Eve was both human help and divine help" (p. 57). Why is this so?

FACE-TO-FACE

13. Write down some of the beliefs you have held concerning the role of woman and how she is to be a help to the man. Some of these beliefs may be of your own construction or they may have been taught to you.

So many of our viewpoints are self-relating. We tend to interpret things as to how they relate to us as human beings, very often from our own understanding of "good and evil." "God, however, is always wanting to move us from a human-centered or self-centered viewpoint to seeing from His perspective—how all things are properly related to Him" (p. 57). Let's look at the word meanings that describe from God's perspective the kind of help the woman would be—the kind of help He deemed to be the solution to a dangerous situation.

When God said, "I will make him an help meet for him," it is actually the word "for" that is our key word.

14. Review and write down the meanings and the root meanings of the word "for" (*nagad*) and the meaning of Eve's name from page 58.

What was God saying about His design of the woman? What was He creating her to be for the man's sake?

How might this affect the man's aloneness?

15. Discuss and respond to the term "face-to-face." What are some words that come to mind when you think of being face-to-face with someone? Write some of them down.

16. What does Dr. Joy state about the differences in structure and function of the brains between male and female that would confirm what God is telling us in Genesis (see pp. 58-59)?

The word for "help" in the Hebrew literally means "to surround and protect." Woman is physically weaker than man so this cannot be referring to physical protection.

17. What part of the man was the woman given by God to surround and protect? (See the last paragraph on page 59 and continuing to the top of page 60.)

18. How might the truths we have discussed in this chapter be applied beyond individual couples to the corporate Church?

A Closer Look at My Own Heart

King Lemuel's mother understood the purpose of woman and counseled her son:

> An excellent [virtuous] wife, who can find? For her worth is far above jewels. The heart of her husband trusts in her, and he will have no lack of gain. She does him good and not evil all the days of her life (Proverbs 31:10-12, *NASB*).

19. If you are a man, consider the following questions:

How does what I have learned today correspond with my attitudes and feelings toward women? (If you are married, consider this question first and foremost in relation to your wife.)

Are there some adjustments in my thinking that need to be made? If so, what are they?

20. If you are a woman, consider the following questions:

How does what I have learned today correspond to my beliefs about myself as a woman?

Does the way I relate to men (particularly my husband, if married) correspond to what I have learned today?

Do some adjustments in my thinking need to be made? If so, what are they?

You may want to discuss these thoughts as a group or write them down.

Action Steps I Can Take Today

We have learned that the design and bringing forth of the woman was a very deliberate and precise act of God for a very definite purpose.

21. Pray and ask the Lord, the One who created us, to give you a fuller revelation of His design and purpose for woman and how man and woman together become one (as in the whole expression of humanity as God designed us).

22. Write down Genesis 5:1,2. Keep it where you can review it often this week. Ask God to renew your mind with this truth.

– Five –

The Strike

Now the serpent was more cunning than any beast of the
field which the Lord God had made. Genesis 3:1

God had great plans for the man and woman He had created and their resulting progeny. It was a powerful plan, beautifully and precisely designed. All of
the universe looked on in wonder. God would rule the earth through His children. As they received His life, they would represent Him in nature and in
authority. The success of the plan depended on their allegiance to God, their
unity and the full expression of who they were—male and female.

Nearly everyone remembers the explosion of the Challenger space shuttle
right after liftoff at Cape Canaveral that fateful day in 1986. So carefully
designed, so powerfully crafted, yet it suddenly blew apart, killing all of the
beloved people aboard. Stunned, people all over the world were asking, "What
happened? What went wrong?"

Our goal in this chapter is to answer a similar question that arises out of a far greater catastrophe. It is to discover the clear tactics of Satan as he over- threw (for a time) God's carefully designed plan for His creation and the dev- astating results in the lives of not only Adam and Eve, but in every man and woman since that time.

A Closer Look at the Problem

God first created the man, observed a problem and then brought forth the woman to help him. Rather than being a help, however, the woman exacer- bated the problem! The design exploded and all that was left was a mere faint resemblance to what God had fashioned. Like those watching the explosion of the Challenger, we often ask, "What happened? How could something so care- fully designed go so terribly awry?" Genesis 3:1 gives us our first clue:

> Now the serpent was more cunning [subtle and crafty] than any beast of the field which the LORD God had made. And he said to the woman, "Has God indeed said, 'You shall not eat of every tree of the garden'?"

Satan is a master tactician. He did not come to Eve with a haphazard plan to just mess things up for God like a child destroying his room while throwing a temper tantrum. He knew exactly what was needed in order for Adam and Eve to fulfill God's mandate for them. He knew he must steer them away from God's provision for them (the tree of life) and toward the tree of the knowledge of good and evil.

1. What have we learned that the tree of the knowledge of good and evil represents?

    Why was it so crucial to Satan that he snare Adam and Eve into eating of the tree of the knowledge of good and evil and not the tree of life?

We know that Satan was successful in his temptation. Both Adam and Eve ate of the tree of the knowledge of good and evil (see Genesis 3:6). It was a coup, a masterstroke, a bull's-eye!

2. Review the last paragraph on page 62, continuing onto page 63. By turn-
    ing Adam and Eve to the tree of the knowledge of good and evil, to what
    did he turn them?

"You Gotta Serve Somebody"

Even though Satan had turned them to self-rule, humanity was never designed
to function independently of a higher power. We merely make the choice by
whom we will be influenced and ruled, even if we are not conscious that we
are doing so. "Do you not know that to whom you present yourselves slaves
to obey, you are that one's slaves whom you obey" (Romans 6:16).

3. While Adam and Eve thought they were choosing independence, in actu-
    ality by whom would they now be ruled (see pp. 63-64)?

Because of Adam's and Eve's choices, a new system was established.

4. Read 2 Corinthians 4:4; 1 John 2:15,16; and 5:19. What is this system called
    and who presides over it (see p. 63)?

"It is important to note that God never intended [that Adam and Eve] should
not know the *difference* between good and evil....God intended for Adam and
Eve, like Jesus, to choose [God's] Spirit (tree of life) as their source of life and
wisdom, rather than their own experience of good and evil" (pp. 63-64).

5. Review the first full paragraph on page 64. Now that Adam and Eve (and
    all who would come after them) were living by their self-centers, from
    what criteria would they arrive at their conclusion of what is good and
    what is evil?

    Pursue this thought further. What are some of the ways those who lean
    on their own understanding pursue good as opposed to evil as they
    develop their lifestyles? (What would influence their choices as they
    design their lives?)

How might this understanding of good and evil as it relates to our own self-centeredness affect the way we view and relate to those of the opposite sex?

Note to Group Leaders: A form of this question will be applied more personally to participants at the end of this chapter under A CLOSER LOOK AT MY OWN HEART.

THE DESIGN DISINTEGRATES

Adam and Eve's choice brought into being the world system over which Satan as the "god of this world" would preside. As such, it shouldn't surprise us that life as it was supposed to be "took a 180-degree turn. The fruit of their action was instantaneous: broken relationship" (p. 64).

> When Satan moved to derail the man and woman, he struck directly at the center of their identities—their maleness and femaleness. It's noteworthy that before Adam and Eve hid themselves from God in the garden they covered themselves from each other; they covered the parts of themselves that identified them as male and female. They became driven by their self-centers. Who they were and how they were designed to function would now become confused, twisted, deceptive, hidden and self-serving (p. 66).

6. Describe some of the ways woman, who was created to be nourished and cherished by the man, is even now being poorly treated, abused or neglected throughout the world (see pp. 64-65). (Add to those noted if you can think of others.)

7. Read the quote by the theologian at the bottom of page 65. In what ways are the seeds of this viewpoint still affecting the church today? Explain.

    Note: Variations of this viewpoint were held by many earlier theologians. If you have some older commentaries (particularly 19th century and earlier) at home or in the church library, it is an interesting exercise to look up their comments on Genesis 3:16 which is their basis for this viewpoint. The goal of this exercise would be to show how relatively recent this perspective toward women in the Church is and to consider the residual effect of this attitude upon us today.

8. "We have seen men—instead of serving their wives and receiving them in the intended place in their lives—seek to use them, objectify them or patronize them" (p. 66). How would this attitude fit right into Satan's objective to destroy the effectiveness of woman and thus the health and well-being of the man (see the last two paragraphs of p. 66)?

   What is Satan's ultimate purpose toward the woman?

9. "Objectify means 'to present (something or someone) as an object; depersonalize them.'"[1] What are some ways men objectify women?

THE DESIRE OF THE WOMAN

The fruit of walking by our own knowledge of what is good and what is evil has been devastating. Not only has man's attitude toward woman been dramatically affected by the Fall but so has woman's attitude toward man. We hear God addressing this very thing as He speaks to Eve, immediately after they partook of the forbidden tree.

10. Read Genesis 3:16. Review and write down both meanings of the word "desire" (*teshuqah*) found on page 68.

Jane states, "This is a key verse for all women. I believe God is revealing to us the root of all dysfunctional behavior in women toward men, and where her heart is most vulnerable to deception. Today we have a new word for it. We call it 'codependence.' God identified it at the beginning of time and called it the 'desire' of the woman" (p. 67).

The words "shall be" in Genesis 3:16 are not actually in the original text.

11. Write down the literal translation of Genesis 3:16 as it relates to the woman's relationship to her husband found in the first paragraph on page 68.

    Discuss and write down what this is saying about the woman's heart attitude toward her husband. (This attitude in the woman's heart extends to the male race in general but becomes specifically focused upon the husband at marriage.)

12. Review the meaning of "objectify" in question 9. What are some ways women objectify men?

OUR "GOD" REIGNS

13. Discuss what it means when we say "our 'god' reigns" (p. 69).

    Do these "gods" reign as an overt action on their part or is it attitude of our own heart? Explain.

    Who, then, holds the key to dethroning these gods and replacing them with the true God?

14. How do we see evidence of the desire of the woman being played out throughout the world (see pp. 69-70.)?

THE BEGINNING OF THE END

15. What is the dream with which women generally enter marriage (see p. 70)?

    Describe what is very often the result in a marriage when this dream is not realized (see p. 71).

Our focus in this chapter has been the problem—the strike. The answer: Only God can fix it. The tear has been too deep and too wide, the devastation too catastrophic. "It will take divine surgery to rectify it" (p. 71).

A Closer Look at My Own Heart

"Now, living from their self-centers, what they judged to be good or evil would be determined by the immediate effect it would have on them. Whatever felt good, or comfortable, or would ensure preeminence, would be good. Pain, discomfort, challenge, [we could add inconvenience, anything that would require self-sacrifice] anything that would diminish self, would be considered evil. All of life would now be ordered from this perspective" (p. 64).

The following questions are not intended to condemn or pass judgment in any way. We are simply attempting to take an honest though perhaps difficult look at our own hearts.

16. Consider your attitudes toward the opposite sex in general and if married, your spouse in particular. Has the way you relate to them been shaped by your own knowledge of good and evil? Is their worth and acceptance to you based mainly on your self-centered perception of how they fit into your life and agenda? Discuss or write down your thoughts.

17. This question is directed specifically to women. Think about the "desire of the woman." Are you looking to your husband to fill up the grand canyon inside of you? One of the ways you can tell is if you struggle with disillusionment, anger and bitterness because of disappointed expectations. Remember, one does not have to be married to be struggling with the aforementioned desire. One can be single and still be looking for that one who will be the answer to life, the one who will make everything OK, meaningful and worthwhile; the one whose approval and affection will deem you a worthy, acceptable person.

Discuss your thoughts with the group or write down your answers.

Action Steps I Can Take Today

Sometimes the only way we can know how we are relating to others is by asking them.

18. If you are married, set up a time to talk with your spouse. Ask if he or she perceives that you are relating to him or her out of your own expectation and personal agenda. Determine not to be offended by the response but to talk it through and attempt to grow through understanding each other.

19. If unmarried, ask one or two close friends to talk through with you the truths in this chapter. Use the time to gain greater perspective of your own expectations and desires toward the opposite gender.

20. Take the whole matter to God in prayer. He will hear you. He has a vested interest in restoring your relationships!

Note:

1. *The American Heritage Dictionary of the English Language, Third Edition* (Boston, Mass.: Houghton Mifflin Co., 1992), Electronic Version.

Six

RIGHT EXPECTATIONS, WRONG SOURCE

For My people have committed two evils: They have
forsaken Me, the fountain of living waters, and hewn themselves cisterns—broken cisterns that can hold no water.
Jeremiah 2:13

Like the stunning, tragic demise of the Challenger space shuttle we mentioned
in the previous chapter, God's beautifully designed plan for His people quickly disintegrated. God's image was corrupted as His design became engulfed in
the flames of self-centeredness. We see the fallout from that explosion all
around us to this day. Jane states:

> We are fashioned for intimacy, we long for love and a sense of true
> caring. Yet, because of the Fall, we live in a world of broken people
> driven by our own needs and self-centers. We move toward others,

based not so much on what they need, but rather on what *we* need, endeavoring somehow to slacken the hidden thirst deep within our souls.

What is the answer to our dilemma then? Are our longings and expectations so unrealistic that they can never be met in this lifetime?

Dr. Reed Davis addresses our question when, in essence, he says, "It is a question of 'source or resource.' God is our source, others in our lives are resources" (pp. 73-74).

1. According to Jeremiah 2:13, anything other than God as our source is what?

Our goal in this chapter is to sort out what God, our Source, intends to be to us. Then, as resources, what He intended husbands and wives (and others) to be to each other. We want to uncover the "broken cisterns" we have fashioned in our lives.

A Closer Look at the Problem

Because of the Fall, we grow up in this world with a skewed perspective as we continually interpret life through the eyes of our own self-centeredness. Before God is able to renew our minds, we have built our lives on false foundations.

It would be wonderful if, once we realize our error, God would simply come in and magically give us a right foundation upon which we could build a satisfying, God-glorifying life.

2. Read the comments by DeVern Fromke at the end of the second paragraph on page 74. What does he say must happen before new foundations can be laid and restoration begins to take place?

EXPOSED FOUNDATIONS

3. What is a false foundation that is being exposed today (see p. 74)?

Why is it important that this foundation be exposed?

4. What are the needs women have that they so desperately want met? Write them down.

    What are these needs called and why?

    Are these legitimate needs?

5. Both men and women have being needs but tend to look to different places to fill them. Where do women tend to look to have their being needs filled?

6. What are some places men tend to look for theirs?

7. Read Genesis 3:17-19. What will be the primary result of Adam's own choice to depend on himself instead of God?

Consider and discuss the implications of the following word meanings:

"In toil you shall eat of [the ground]" (v. 17). Toil: "worrisome, i.e. labor or pain, sorrow, toil."[1] "Refers to physical pain as well as emotional sorrow."[2]

"In the sweat of your face you shall eat bread" (v. 19). Sweat: "as caused by agitation and fear."[3]

What do the words "labor," "pain," "sorrow," "toil," "agitation" and "fear" tell us about how a man who does not depend on God as his source would relate to his work? Why do you think this is so?

How might this anxiety and turmoil concerning his work affect a man's relationships?

UNCOVERING THE SNARE

8. According to the first paragraph under this subheading in the book, what was Satan's goal in his temptation of Adam and Eve (see pp. 74-75.)?

"All of us live life from what we truly believe. It is not what we think or know intellectually, but what we are convinced of in our hearts that directs and guides our lives—our actions and reactions. Ultimately, our heart-held beliefs will be evidenced by our behavior" (p. 75).

9. Read Larry Crabb's statement on page 75. What determines our goals and expectations?

The desire (*teshuqah*) of the woman "is a deep inner longing that is 'turning away,' and 'stretching out after' the man."

"Remember, this was not part of the curse. God was uncovering a snare to Eve. Because she was turning away from the living God, the one true source of life, she would now be ruled by the false source of life to which she was turning" (p. 75).

10. What will the things we think will satisfy our longing become to us (see p. 76)?

11. Why is "satisfaction found in a wrong source or false god...always temporary" (p. 76)?

How are we controlled by these false gods, i.e., "broken cisterns"?

EVIDENCE OF EXPECTATIONS

"The desire of the woman is a heart-held belief. It is the belief that her husband can be her source of life, that he can meet her need for unfailing love, worth, security and purpose" (p. 76). Our heart-held beliefs will be evidenced by our behavior.

12. What behavior in the woman is evidence of this heart-held belief?

13. Because the woman is looking to her husband for her life (her being needs), what will be the result to her? (See the third paragraph under "Evidence of Expectations," p. 76.)

SPIRITUAL ADULTERY

14. What is adultery (see definition on p. 77)?

    What is spiritual adultery?

James 4:1-4 describes for us how strife originates. This passage of Scripture vividly describes the result when we look to others rather than God to have our needs met. "This is the way that leads to death as far as relationship is concerned" (p. 78).

15. Read James 4:1-4 (*AMP*) found on page 77. What do these verses tell us happens when our expectations are not met in the way we want?

    What happens to our hearts (see p. 78)?

16. When we behave in this way, "from God's point of view we have turned from Him, the true source of life, to seek out other 'lovers' who we think will satisfy the longing of our souls" (p. 78). What does James call this?

A Closer Look at God's Truth

RIGHT EXPECTATIONS, RIGHT SOURCE

"God wants to rectify in each of us the disastrous effects of our heritage in Adam and Eve. We are still unwittingly eating the fruit of their wrong choice." The evidence in our marriages tells us that many of us are still eating from the wrong tree. "It is God's ultimate intention to move us from the tree of the knowledge of good and evil—that which we seek in our own understanding to give meaning and worth to our lives—to the tree of life, God Himself" (p. 78).

17. Read the quote from DeVern Fromke on page 78. What does Fromke say must take place before we can live life by our new source—God?

Unless we become aware of how much we are still living life from the old tree we will not truly be cut loose from it. We will not sense our need for this divine surgery.

18. On page 78 we see the being needs listed again. In the same paragraph, what are we told happens to our relationships when we find our life, our being needs, in God?

Explain why we are able to move in true intimacy with others once we have found our life in God.

A DIVINE TURNING

On pages 78-79, Jane states, "I want to emphasize strongly that none of what I have said here is intended to negate the fact that many legitimate needs must be met in the marriage relationship for it to function properly. Many critical changes may be needed."

19. Two kinds of needs are mentioned in the paragraph at the top of page 79. What are these needs and what is the difference between the two?

20. "What makes [a woman] vulnerable to the deception [that her husband should meet all of her needs] is that what she wants is 'good,' even necessary" (p. 79). Read Genesis 3:6. How do we see this vulnerability to being deceived by good demonstrated in Eve's life?

    Were all of the things the tree of the knowledge of good and evil offered things that God did not want Eve to have? What was the real issue here?

21. The source from which Eve obtained these things was the real issue with God. "Right things from the wrong source constitute lust. The desire of the woman springs from this root; it is a form of lust" (p. 79). Why is the desire of the woman a form of lust?

22. Describe what happens to a woman when she sets her desire back on God (see bottom paragraph on pp. 79-80)?

"When the woman stops looking to her husband for the needs he cannot meet, she frees him to meet the ones he can" (p. 80). This dynamic also applies to a husband in relationship with his wife.

23. What are the needs God intends husbands and wives to meet in each other?

    How does this principle apply in our relationships with others (children, friends, coworkers, etc.)?

A DOOR UNLOCKS

On page 80 and following, Jane shares her story about the incredible freedom that came to her and her husband, Howard, when they gave up their heart-held beliefs that caused each of them, but particularly Jane, to look to the other as their source of life. Even though Jane had extended much forgiveness for past hurts, she found she was still not free in her relationship with Howard. It was through a fresh understanding of the parable of the debt in Matthew 18:22-35 that she saw it was not only the past debt she must forgive but the daily debt of their relationship, the new expectations that surfaced every day.

"We tend to see the debts others owe us—especially our mates—as much bigger than our own. Surely we have done more, loved better, tried harder than they have" (p. 81).

24.   To whose debt does God compare our debt (see p. 81)?

25.   Read Matthew 18:29,34. What was the ultimate state of both servants and how does this apply to us?

Even though the first servant knew he had been completely forgiven of his debt, he didn't fully understand how entirely impossible it was for him to pay it—"Have patience with me, and I will pay you all" (Matthew 18:29)—and how utterly dependent he was on the grace and mercy of the king.

26.   How does the way we view ourselves before God affect the way we relate to others?

A Closer Look at My Own Heart

First Timothy 6:17 says, "[Do not] trust in uncertain riches but in the living God who gives us richly all things to enjoy." Jane quotes "a wise teacher...'You can tell when you have put your hope in things—riches, people, home, cars, etc.—you stop enjoying them. When we put our hope in God, we enjoy Him and other things as well'" (p. 78).

27.   Think about all the things mentioned above—riches, people, home, cars, etc. We should also add "work." Is there anything or anyone you have stopped enjoying that you know God intends for you to enjoy? Write down whatever or whoever comes to mind.

There may be other things you are still attempting to find your enjoyment in, but you know that ultimately they will never bring the satisfaction to your soul you are looking for. Write these things down as well.

Note: The things on your list are good clues that will lead you to the discovery of some of your "broken cisterns"—containers that cannot hold water.

If there is time share your thoughts with your group.

Action Steps I Can Take Today

God never shows us a truth to condemn us, only to bring us to the place where, through repentance and prayer, we will ask Him to do what only He can—perform open-heart surgery.

28. Come before the Lord with an open heart. Tell Him that you have made for yourself broken cisterns and the water you were seeking to satisfy your soul has long since leaked out.

    Tell the Lord what your broken cisterns are. Ask Him to forgive you for making these persons or things "gods" to whom you have looked to give you life, meaning and security.

29. Write John 4:14 on a card and put it where you can see it this week.

As you meditate on this verse, ask the Lord to give you a fresh revelation of Himself as the "water of life" and His intention to abundantly satisfy you now, in this life, and in the one to come.

Notes:

1. James Strong, *Strong's Exhaustive Concordance* (Grand Rapids, Mich.: Baker Book House, 1984), #6093, p. 90.
2. Editors: R. Laird Harris, Gleason L. Archer Jr. and Bruce K. Waltke, *Theological Wordbook of the Old Testament* (Chicago: Moody Press, 1980), #1666, p. 687.
3. *Strong's*, #2188 and root #2111, p. 35.

- *Seven* -

HIDDEN MAN OF THE HEART

———•◦◦◦•———

As in water face answereth to face, so the heart of
man to man. Proverbs 27:19 (*KJV*)

———•◦◦◦•———

In chapter 6 we uncovered one of the greatest barriers to intimacy—viewing our relationships with others as "sources" of life rather than the "resources" God has given us for our growth and good. Only God can be our Source of life. It is as we find our identity, worth, purpose, security and unfailing love in Him that we will gain the courage to risk reaching out beyond ourselves to connect more deeply with others on a consistent basis.

Having established that God intended people to be merely resources in our lives, free now from grasping after them for what they cannot give us, we are ready to look more closely at what intimacy is and how we can begin to move toward this deeper level of relationship. Such are our goals in this chapter.

A Closer Look at the Problem

One of the most common complaints and the source of much disappointment, grief and pain in women worldwide is the emotional absence of their husbands—to them and to their families. No amount of busyness or determination to find satisfaction in other things will quench this deep longing in women.

> "The fact of the matter is, God didn't intend for it to!" Jane asserts. "God designed woman with an inner need to have an intimate relationship with her husband, one that goes deeper than just the sexual relationship, which at first seemed enough by itself.
>
> "At precisely this point, many, if not most, marriages break down. Multitudes divorce. Others, many of them Christians who do not believe in divorce, get stuck here. Unless they discover God's plan and purpose for them, they will live for years in quiet desperation and pain" (pp. 85-86).

THE HONEYMOON IS OVER

1. Describe what we mean when we say, "The honeymoon is over" when speaking of newly married couples (see p. 86).

   Explain what often begins to happen within a woman after a few months of marriage.

   Describe what is often a husband's response to this turn of events.

The task-oriented young man in the counselor's office complained that he didn't know what his wife wanted from him. "I'm responsible," he told the counselor. "I come home every night, I bring home my paycheck. I'm committed to this marriage!" (p. 87).

2. What was the counselor's response and what do you think he meant by it?

    Pursue this thought further. What is the difference between being committed to a principle or an institution and being committed to a person? How would this affect the relationship?

3. What is the woman really saying to her husband when she says things like "You don't really care about me" or "I want a relationship with you"?

4. Gary Smalley says, "Women have a marriage manual in their hearts." What do you think he means by this statement?

5. God often uses the "unrest and dissatisfaction with the status quo in the woman's heart to move the couple to their next level of growth" (p. 87). What is it that is crucial at this point in the marriage?

A Closer Look at God's Truth

MOVING ON

"George Guilder…writes that woman's sexuality is far more relational than man's. He calls it 'long-term' sexuality" (p. 87).

6. Read Guilder's quote following the above sentence on page 87. Respond to his statement. What do you think he means?

7. What is it that makes women more relational (see the last line on page 87 continuing to page 88)?

8. Although "we should not be controlled by feelings or depend on them as an infallible source of truth" (p. 88), what is it that our feelings and emotions will tell us about ourselves as we begin to process them?

"As in water face answereth to face, so the heart of man to man [one human being to another]" (Proverbs 27:19, *KJV*).

9. What happens in the mirrored effect—the face-to-face dynamic—of relationship?

How would the woman's ability to more readily identify and process emotions affect her husband if she is received on this open and transparent level?

FASHIONED FOR INTIMACY

The book of 1 Peter is written to "Christians living in various parts of Asia Minor who are suffering rejection in the world because of their obedience to Christ"[1] (4:1-4,12-16).

10. Read 1 Peter 3:1-6 as quoted on page 89. Then read 1 Peter 2:21-23 and 3:8-10 which bracket this passage and provide its context. Note that these latter two passages refer to Jesus' behavior as our example to follow. Was Jesus always silent (i.e., used no words) in His interaction with His detractors (see p. 90)?

How did He respond to them?

11. Is 1 Peter 3:1 telling us that a woman is not to use any words at all in her relationship with her husband? In context, what is it telling us?

12. We are told that the woman's submission is to be as one who is adorned with "the hidden person of the heart." What is the scriptural meaning of the word "heart" (see bottom of p. 90)?

How would a woman who is adorned with "the hidden person of the heart" relate to her husband?

Note: First Peter 3:8 begins a long summary of all that Peter has just said in his instructions, starting with servants (2:18), then wives (3:1) and finally husbands (3:7). This is a summary of how we all are to live and relate to one another.

BE PREPARED FOR REACTIONS

Living in true relationship takes wisdom and courage. First Peter 3:6 admonishes the woman not to be "afraid with any terror" (p. 91).

13. Review the meaning of the word "terror" on page 91. What could cause a woman to feel terror as she begins to share her heart with her husband?

14. Review the quote from John and Paula Sandford beginning on page 91. What do they explain is the cause for a husband's attack on overtures of intimacy from his wife?

    Explore this further. What do you think of the Sandfords' explanation?

"The woman in 1 Peter 3 is being exhorted to live with her husband as one who has learned to trust in God [see v. 5]" (p. 92).

15. Read 1 Peter 3:6. Correlate verse 6 with verse 14, part of Peter's summary to all which says, "But even if you should suffer for the sake of righteousness, you are blessed. And do not fear their intimidation, and do not be troubled" (*NASB*). Explain what these verses tell us should be the attitude of anyone, man or woman, who trusts in God in the face of rebuffs, angry response or suffering.

    How will a woman who has learned to trust in God respond to her husband? (See Proverbs 31:26 and other Scripture verses quoted in the last two paragraphs on pp. 92-93.)

    Describe how the woman's example might help her husband (see pp. 93-94).

RULES OR RELATIONSHIP?

God's goal is always relationship but not relationship at any cost. It must be relationship without guile or deceit (see 1 Peter 3:10), founded on mercy—which springs from love—and truth. Love is critical, but love without truth is not genuine love, it is manipulative and self-serving. On the other hand, truth without love will destroy—"the letter kills" (2 Corinthians 3:6)—rather than heal and bring life.

"This is true submission 'as unto the Lord.' It is more about relationship than it is about authority" (p. 93). "Submission is [the woman] knowing her purpose from God's viewpoint and then bringing her whole self to the man for his good, knowing that their destiny is together" (p. 94).

16. What would be the difference between rule-oriented submission and relationship-oriented submission?

17. Considering Sarah and Abraham's life together as a whole, what kind of a relationship did they have?

ACCORDING TO UNDERSTANDING

According to 1 Peter 3:7, a "man is to understand his wife, the nature and design God has given her for his help" (p. 94).

18. How is the man to treat his wife, and why?

19. "It is true that only God can give the husband 'life' in the eternal sense, but the woman can lead him into life so that even eternal things take on a greater significance for him" (p. 94). Explain how a woman can draw a man "into life" and how this might affect his eternal good.

20. Review the quotes from Paul Tournier and John Powell on page 95. What will happen to us if we remain hidden and self-protective?

REAL MEN DO

"All of life seems to conspire in keeping the man in a hidden and thus emotionally [closed] condition" (p. 95).

21. Review the quote from Daphne Kingma beginning on page 95. Explain how life and society conspire to keep men emotionally closed.

22. What are some strategies men have learned from childhood to protect themselves from emotions that would label them unmanly or unmasculine (see p. 96)?

23. What is the danger, the cost, to men for their self-protectiveness?

24. In order to have a true relationship with someone, what must we bring? Why?

25. Describe the ripple effect of man's isolation on society at every level.

26. "A man whose heart has begun to trust his wife will gain courage to share with her the wounds and failures of the past" (p. 96). (See Proverbs 31:11.) Describe what God intends to happen within the emotional intimacy of relationships, particularly in, but not limited to, marriage.

A Closer Look at My Own Heart

One man, struggling mightily to take his God-ordained role as a full participator in his family, said, "How could I know that my family had emotional needs when I didn't know I had them myself?"

This may be the case in your life. You can't begin to meet the emotional needs of others until you get in touch with your own and begin to process them.

27. In light of the cost of the emotional abandonment of their families by men (and some women), consider whether you have fully entered into this dimension in your life and the lives of others to whom you have a relational responsibility.

28. Women, have you fully understood your role as a help in your husband's life, or have you succumbed, more often than not, to discouragement and perhaps the fear that comes with his rebuffs?

Discuss these questions as a group or simply hold your conversation with God and write down your answers.

Action Steps I Can Take Today

29. Pray for greater sensitivity to your own feelings and those of others around you. Ask for wisdom to communicate in nonthreatening ways and courage to break through your own self-protective ways.

30. Knowing that you are secure in God, that He is your Source and you no longer need to fear what people can do to you, make a verbal commitment to someone—to your spouse if you are married—to begin being more honest and open with him or her.

    This will take time. Commit to a specific time to be with this person on a consistent, frequent basis. Schedule activities that will be conducive to meaningful conversation.

Note:
1. Jack Hayford, Editor, *Spirit-Filled Life Bible* (Nashville, Tenn.: Thomas Nelson Publishers, 1991), p. 1905.

- Eight -

UNMASKING THE ACCUSER

"The accuser of our brethren…has been cast down."
Revelation 12:10

In this chapter we will pursue another barrier to intimacy. This one is related to the first—seeing others as our source of life—but it warrants special attention. As we begin to share ourselves with others, we will find ourselves fleeing back into our hiding places deep within us if we don't understand the principle of this chapter. This is a favorite tactic of the enemy, one that showed its deceptive face in the very first temptation in the garden. It has a name. It is called false shame and it is essential that we gain a grasp of this favorite weapon of Satan so that we may disempower him in our lives.

The goal in this session is to gain discernment between false shame and true shame so that we may walk free from both.

A Closer Look at the Problem

CHECKED YOUR ID LATELY?

Someone has said, "Children are terrific observers but terrible interpreters." They are quick to notice everything going on around them but their interpretation of those events, if left to themselves, will be woefully lacking.

Extremely egocentric, children tend to interpret life as being all about them. They are not capable of accurately evaluating the validity of the words and actions of others, no matter how inappropriate. Like sponges, children soak it all in as gospel truth, as judgments about their identity and value. When bad things are spoken or done to children, they are most likely to believe it is because they are bad people.

All of us were children and all of us, for the most part, are still dealing with the negative messages we interpreted as being the truth about ourselves from our earliest days.

1. Read the sixth paragraph on page 100. Messages come to us in many ways and from many fronts. What are some of the different ways we receive messages about ourselves?

    What are some of the messages that we receive?

2. "It is normal to form our pictures of ourselves from the messages we receive around us. God intended it to be that way—that who we are would be mirrored by others in our lives, affirmed and confirmed by them" (p. 100). What went wrong with God's plan?

    As a result, what kind of inner picture do most of us have of ourselves and why is it so essential that we be healed? (See the second paragraph on page 101.)

THE THIEF OF INTIMACY

"Enter the master tactician" (p. 101).

3. What is Satan's intent in crippling us in our youth?

4. Review the meanings of "Satan" and "devil" on page 102. Since this is his nature, how can we identify his voice in our lives?

Remember that Satan's goal for Adam's and Eve's lives was to turn them from being God-focused to being self-focused. "He knew that if he could turn them to themselves, they would have no power against him, and he would be safe....Although we are on the other side of redemption, Satan uses the same tactic. If he can't steal our salvation, he knows he can cripple us for God's purposes if he can again cause us to become self-focused" (p. 102).

5. When the serpent "came to ensnare Eve by pointing out that the fruit from the forbidden tree...would make her 'be like God,'" what was he implying (see the last two paragraphs on p. 102)?

6. Write down the essence of Satan's message to Eve from the top of page 103. This is the "shame message" that we hear every time we are feeling inadequate even though we are not always able to articulate the words.[1]

    Part of this message was true and part of it was lies. Which was which?

Eve believed the lies and the implication that there was something wrong with "not being enough." "She reached out with her own hands to make up the deficit she perceived to be in her. Adam soon followed...by focusing on themselves, the bridge between them and their true Source of Life was broken."

"Now, wholly dependent upon themselves, what had been only a perceived deficiency became a true one. They were naked...exposed...in danger of being rejected and abandoned forever" (p. 103).

Two Kinds of Shame

7. Read Revelation 3:17,18. What does verse 18 say we'll feel if we are found naked and exposed with the resulting danger of being rejected and abandoned?

8. Why does God allow us to feel this sense of legitimate shame that is the result of going our own way, and what is His remedy for it (see p. 104)?

9. There is another kind of shame. What is it called and how does it make us feel?

"This is 'false shame,' the precursor [forerunner] of sin" (p. 104). False shame is Satan's attempt to convince us there is something wrong with us when there isn't in order to cause us, like Adam and Eve, to take things into our own hands and add to ourselves whatever we think is lacking. "Satan came to Eve with this lie [that it was unacceptable to be insufficient] before the Fall, before there was any sin, and after our sins are forgiven, he comes to us telling the same lie" (p. 104).

10. Soon after our salvation, Satan comes again to us. It is a familiar voice and we think the thoughts are ours, but they are really his. What does he whisper to our minds and what is the result?

11. "The message of false shame is not connected with sinful things we have done" (p. 105). What is false shame? (See the first paragraph on page 105.)

12. Review or write down the quote from Keith Miller. Have you ever felt this way? Elaborate.

HIDE AND SEEK

13. Once we decide we are flawed, unacceptable and irreparably defective, what becomes our game and how do we play it?

What is your hiding place—the behavior you find yourself reverting to when you become fearful that someone may find the real you?

14. Read Isaiah 28:20, *Amplified*, as quoted at the top of page 106. Describe how this verse relates to our dilemma.

THE BAGGAGE WE BRING

15. "Many of us bring this mentality, this distorted, self-focused, defective view of ourselves into our relationships—perhaps most significantly that of marriage—along with the accompanying masks" (p. 106). How would this affect our marriages?

On pages 106-108 Jane describes the self-perceptions and the accompanying masks both she and Howard brought into their marriage.

16. Read the quote from Don Hudson on page 107. Howard related well to Don's words. How do you (or others in the group) relate to his words?

    Pursue this further. How have you personally responded to your sense of deficiency as you have related to the world around you?

Both Howard and Jane attempted to make up their sense of inadequacy in different ways. Howard appeared confident, friendly and happy. Yet he was so insecure that any overtures toward him for intimacy or request for change in the status quo would be met with anger and intimidation.

17. Read Proverbs 18:19. How does this truth apply to Howard and the many others like him?

    What happens to the person who builds impenetrable defenses to keep others out (see p. 108)?

Jane majored in perfection—being the best at everything. Yet she could do nothing to make her marriage measure up to her perfect standard. She saw this as a personal failure which caused her to focus even more on Howard's behavior.

18. The parable of the unforgiving servant in Matthew 18 reveals a profound dynamic. Read the account on page 108. Neither asked for forgiveness. What did they ask for and why?

    What does this reveal about them?

    Describe the end result.

A Closer Look at God's Truth

UNLOVE

Nancy Groom, in her book *Marriage Without Masks*, calls all of our self-seeking striving "unlove."

19. Read the passage from Nancy Groom's book on page 109. What does Nancy say is the root sin in our lives for which we must repent before we can begin to repent of our failure to love others?

20. Nancy declares, "Repentance involves two things." What are they?

21. Why will our commitment to "staying safe" in our marriages and other relationships hinder what God wants to accomplish in our lives?

IN DYING, WE LIVE

What is the answer to this terrifying sense of insufficiency from which all of us have suffered? Is it the self-affirmation we so often hear about—pasting positive statements about ourselves on the bathroom mirror, "hoping that if we say them often enough we will finally believe them" (p. 110)?

22. What is the answer to our sense of insufficiency?

The very thing Don Hudson was terrified of, admitting his deficiency, is the very thing God is after in all of us. It will mean "death" to us, just as Don feared, but it is the right kind of death: death to looking to ourselves and others as our source of life and acceptance; death to our self-dependence.

23. Read Luke 9:23,24. How do these verses relate to the above truth?

24. "The message that tripped up Eve was not merely that she was insufficient, but also her interpretation that, as such, her condition was flawed and unacceptable" (p. 110). What is the difference between being insufficient and being defective?

Write down or discuss in what ways you are insufficient.

What is God's design for us and why has He designed us so?

It is true that as fallen creatures we are defective. Satan's deceptive tactic, however, was to try to convince Eve that she was defective before she fell because in herself she was insufficient. After we're saved, forgiven and declared righteous in Jesus Christ, Satan continues to approach us with this same lie—that we need to be more than we are in order to be acceptable. His goal is always to focus us on ourselves which inevitably causes us to come up short. The real issue is not who we are but who God is and who we are in Him.

25. When we are free of our masks in the body of Christ, what will happen (see p. 110)?

A Closer Look at My Own Heart

26. Think about the ways you have "played the game" of staying safe in life, of staying out of pain by protecting yourself in any way you can. Write down whatever comes to mind.

27. To whom are we devoted when we play such games and upon whom are we depending?

28. The purpose of masks is to make ourselves acceptable to others, which means we are still looking to people as our source of life. Are you ready to begin the journey of trusting God for your life enough to start removing some of the masks you wear that separate you from others as the Holy Spirit makes you aware of them? If not, why not?

Action Steps I Can Take Today

29. Ask the Lord to reveal your masks to you and how they originated. Spend some time thinking about and writing down some of the messages you received about yourself as a child and what masks you consequently constructed to make yourself acceptable. Make a list as the Holy Spirit brings them to mind.

30. Go to the person with whom you have committed to become more open and honest. Ask him or her to make this list the subject of your next meeting together. Bring your list, share your reasons for your particular masks and pray together for healing and freedom.

Note:
1. For a more in-depth study of the subject of false shame see the Aglow Bible study *Shame: Thief of Intimacy*, Marie Powers (Ventura. Calif.: Gospel Light, 1998).

- Nine -

A SNARE, A FETTER OR A CROWN?

*I applied my heart to know, to search and seek out wisdom
and the reason of things, to know the wickedness of folly,
even of foolishness and madness. And I find more bitter than
death the woman whose heart is snares and nets, whose
hands are fetters. Ecclesiastes 7:25,26*

King Solomon, who had at least 1000 wives and concubines and was the writer of the book of Ecclesiates, knew whereof he spoke. Herbert Lockyer, in his book *All the Women of the Bible*, observes, "No man has ever lived who has had as much experience with women as King Solomon, who 'loved many [idolatrous] women.'"[1] King Solomon knew firsthand the influence of women. Sadly though, through his own choices, he knew more about their influence for evil than for good.

We have studied in previous chapters about the powerful influence God designed women to have in the lives of their husbands. In this chapter our goal is to more clearly define what kind of influence women are to be.

A Closer Look at the Problem

THE INFLUENCE OF WOMEN

The Bible declares that "King Solomon surpassed all the kings of the earth in riches and wisdom" (1 Kings 10:23). He was the wisest man in all the earth, anointed so by God. There had not been anyone like him before his time nor did anyone like him arise after him. He began his ministry with a "wise and understanding heart" (1 Kings 3:12), a deep love and dependence on the Lord. Yet there came a day when "the LORD became angry with Solomon, because his heart had turned from the LORD God of Israel," so that God announced, "'I will surely tear the kingdom away from you'" (11:9,11).

1. Read 1 Kings 11:1-4. What is it that turned the heart of King Solomon, the wisest man in the history of the earth, from God and thus brought him to spiritual ruin?

"God intended [the woman's] influence to be felt, but God was after influence for 'good and not evil'" (Proverbs 31:12). She was to be a help "as to the Lord" (Ephesians 5:22) (see p. 115). Let's look more closely at what we mean by this.

GOOD OR EVIL?

2. Review and write down the definition of good and evil from page 115.

In *Fashioned for Intimacy* much is said about the self-center as the source of sin and thus evil, even though the actions of such a person do not always fit what we would define as evil. His or her actions may even appear "right" and "good" and have "good reason" behind them. Remember the tree of the knowledge of good and evil looked "good." "There is a way that seems right to a man, but its end is the way of death," we are told in Proverbs 14:12.

3. Self-centeredness (the self as the center, source and the focus of life) is idolatry. What is idolatry at its core? Who are we really worshiping? Explain. (See p. 115.)

The worship of other gods (people, money, power, etc.) is merely an effort to manipulate life so that it serves oneself. A woman who is devoted to her own agenda, who is attempting to manipulate life so that it serves her, is described by Solomon as "more bitter than death" and one "whose heart is snares and nets, whose hands are fetters." The effectiveness of Solomon's life "especially as it relates to God's kingdom, was greatly diminished" (p. 116) by his love for such self-devoted women.

THE EVIL WOMAN

In Scripture an evil, idolatrous woman is symbolized by the term "harlot."

4. "In God's eyes, harlotry is not limited to sexual promiscuity" (p. 116). Describe what harlotry is symbolic of in Scripture.

Is it possible to be a Christian woman and yet be seeking satisfaction apart from God's life and ways? Explain.

5. Review the list of characteristics of an idolatrous woman on pages 116-117 and look up the accompanying scriptures. Discuss ways that even Christian women may indulge in behaviors symbolized in these verses.

What is the purpose of this behavior?

What kind of influence is this and why?

A Closer Look at God's Truth

THE GODLY WOMAN

The characteristics of the godly woman are in direct opposition to those of the evil woman. We can find the qualities of the godly woman in 1 Peter 3.

6. Six characteristics are listed on pages 116-118 for both the evil woman and the godly woman. As you review the qualities of the godly woman, draw the following chart in your notebook, then complete it (the first row is completed as an example).

Characteristic	The Evil Woman	The Godly Woman
Her words	*flatters with her words to ensure her own agenda is met*	*responsible with her words—neither flatters nor severely criticizes*
Her sexuality		
Her motives/methods		
Her level of satisfaction with life		
Her source of satisfaction		
Her stability		

Look up the accompanying scriptures (remember the context of 1 Peter 3:1 as discussed in chapter 7). As you consider each point, discuss some ways you think the godly woman lives out these truths and perhaps some of the difficulties she may encounter as the possible cost of her behavior.

7. Note the third quality of the godly woman. "She does not withhold sex to 'punish' her husband, and she does not engage in sex to 'appease' her husband" (p. 117). Both of these responses are manipulative and self-protective. Why is this so?

8. The godly woman "influences for good" (p. 118). What is the purpose of this kind of influence and how does God view it?

Too Soon Old, Too Late Smart

No doubt King Solomon eventually understood the folly of his choices in women but such knowledge came too late in his life to do him any good. This doesn't have to happen to us. Whether we are male or female, it will be of great benefit for us to truly understand what a virtuous (godly) woman is. Proverbs 31 is a good place to start:

9. Look up Proverbs 3:13-15 and 8:11. Notice the similarity of these verses with 31:10. Putting these verses together, what can we conclude about the value God places on the godly woman?

"The heart of her husband safely trusts her; so he will have no lack of gain" (Proverbs 31:11).

"Scripture frequently speaks of putting our trust solely in God: 'Trust in Him [the Lord] at all times, you people; pour out your heart before Him; God is a refuge for us' (Psalm 62:8). Yet here in Proverbs we are told that a man who has found a godly wife can also safely trust his heart to her" (p. 118).

10. What is the meaning of "safely trust" (see bottom of p. 118)?

11. Notice how closely Psalm 62:8 and the full meaning of Proverbs 31:11 resemble each other. What is God saying here about the virtuous, or godly, woman?

12. Review the meaning of the word "heart" and the comments that follow at the top of page 119. How is the godly woman a safe haven for her husband's heart and how is this lived out in their lives?

13. Read Genesis 2:25. This was God's original design for man and woman in marriage. How does this verse symbolically apply to question 13?

14. A man who has found a godly wife will "lack no gain," or as the *NIV* says it, "He will lack nothing of value" (Proverbs 31:11). In your estimation what do you think is really valuable or gain in this life?

15. "She does him good and not evil all the days of her life" (Proverbs 31:12). "Good is what proceeds from God" (p. 115) and "that which draws God-ward" (p. 120). How does the godly woman live out verse 12 (see the top of p. 120)?

16. "She opens her mouth with wisdom, and on her tongue is the law of kindness. She watches over the ways of her household" (Proverbs 31:26,27). Much teaching on Proverbs 31 has focused only on a woman's "physical labor and financial prowess," limiting the woman "to her many household tasks" (p. 120). Review the meaning of the word "watches" (*tsaphah*). Describe its meaning and how it applies to the godly woman.

17. "She seeks wool and flax, and willingly works with her hands" (Proverbs 31:13). Review the meanings of "wool" and "flax" on page 121. Apply the symbolism of this verse to the godly woman—what is she doing with her hands?

18. How do the hands of the godly woman compare to the hands of the evil woman?

19. Read Proverbs 31:21. What is the basis of this woman's confidence (see p. 122.)?

20. "She is like the merchant ships, she brings her food from afar" (Proverbs 31:14). What kind of food is symbolized here and how does the godly woman accomplish this?

21. "Strength and honor are her clothing; she shall rejoice in time to come" (Proverbs 31:25). Review the meaning of the word "rejoice" and the accompanying comments. What is the basis of the woman's laughter and her confidence in the future?

A SNARE, A FETTER OR A CROWN?

22. Read Proverbs 12:4 as quoted on page 123 and review the meanings of "rottenness" and "bones" on page 124. As a summary of the influence for evil, describe the effect on her husband of the woman who "causes [him] shame."

Notice that the man who has been made ashamed by his wife has not necessarily become a thief, a murderer or a publisher of pornography, but his strength has been eroded so that his potential is never fulfilled. This is not to say that the woman has the responsibility for her husband's life and choices but she is an extremely significant influence for strength or weakness in his life.

23. The godly or virtuous woman, however, is a "crown" to her husband. "Crowns relate to wisdom" (p. 124). (See Proverbs 4:9.) What is the meaning of the word "crown" and how can we apply it to the meaning of the word "helper" in Genesis 2:18?

Proverbs 31:11 says that a man's heart may safely trust in a virtuous woman. "Heart" is alternately translated as "understanding" in the Old Testament. "Wisdom and understanding are seated in the heart."[2] "God has uniquely and specifically designed the woman to influence her husband's understanding more profoundly than any other person in his life." In doing so "she will bring him honor: 'a crown'" (p. 124).

The influence of the godly woman will be felt in the man's life far outside the four walls of his home and their own intimate relationship.

24. Read Proverbs 31:23. What is the ripple effect of the woman's influence in her husband's life?

25. Considering the awesome place God has given to women, how do you think Satan responds to her?

A Closer Look at My Own Heart

As we have discovered, Scripture has much to say about the immense value and the incredible role God intends women to play in His design for man, for family and ultimately society. We will further address her role as a prayer warrior in chapter 10. As we conclude this chapter we want to focus on the influence of the woman, particularly in marriage.

God has fashioned all of us for intimacy but the woman particularly so. As such, her influence will be felt in the very depths of her husband's being, in his understanding and in his emotions—for good or for evil. Consider the following questions before the Lord:

26. Women: Are you aware of the extent of the power of influence you exert in the life of your husband?

    Are you willing to leave your safe place, your self-protective ways and become fully present to your husband even if it is uncomfortable for a time?

    Will you take the mantle and become the crown to him that God designed you to be?

27. Men: Have you received your wife as the help, the influence God intended you to have through her or have you been keeping her at a distance, guarding yourself against the very blessing that will help bring wholeness and healing to your life?

A Snare, a Fetter or a Crown?

Are you willing to leave your safe place, your self-protective ways and become fully present to your wife even if it is uncomfortable for a time?

Will you receive her from God's hand as a precious gift to you?

Perhaps you feel unable to adequately respond to the above heart searching questions. Perhaps you feel you have lived in your self-protective ways too many years and you don't know how to emerge from your hiding place, whether you are a man or a woman.

God said, "It is not good that the man should be alone; I will make him an help meet [suitable] for him" (Genesis 2:18, *KJV*). Therefore, if you are a woman, you can trust Him to make you the suitable help He promised. If you are a man, you can trust God to enable you to receive the help He has made for you.

Action Steps I Can Take Today

28. Bring your fears of inadequacy to the Lord. Tell Him you are trusting Him to fulfill His own perfect design in your life.

29. Talk with your spouse. Share your fears, your doubts, and ask him or her to support you in prayer as you make this new commitment before the Lord. Commit to be patient and give each other grace as you learn to walk this new road.

30. Write down Proverbs 18:22. Ask God to give you a heart revelation of His intent for you as you meditate on this verse throughout the week.

Notes:

1. Herbert Lockyer, *All the Women of the Bible* (Grand Rapids: Zondervan Publishing House, 1988), p. 270.
2. *Theological Wordbook of the Old Testament* (Chicago: The Moody Bible Institute, 1980), #1071a, p. 466.

83

- Ten -

THE WARRIOR WOMAN

And I will put enmity between you and the woman, and
between your seed and her Seed; He shall bruise your head,
and you shall bruise His heel. Genesis 3:15

As God spoke these words, the most devastating and catastrophic event ever to affect humanity had just taken place. God Himself had been betrayed by the pinnacle of His creation, man and woman. Surely He would be so angry that He would wipe them out with a breath! Yet, right in the beginning, God responded with the same intrinsic quality He displays toward His people over and over again throughout Scripture. He speaks of His plans for recovery.

Our goal in this chapter is to show how the woman, though deceived and beguiled into behavior that was the exact opposite of God's design for her—helping the man toward death rather than life—would ultimately be instrumental in the final and total demise of her antagonist and God's, Satan himself.

A Closer Look at the Problem

Satan had made a giant inroad by deceiving Eve and as God pronounces the consequences of this history altering event, he is the first to be addressed.

1. Even though Satan had been successful in his first strike, in essence what is God telling him in Genesis 3:15 (see p. 127)?

Notice God's immediate response to the situation.

2. Describe God's way of dealing with conflict and defeat in our lives.

3. "In the net which they hid, their own foot is caught" (Psalm 9:15). How does this verse apply to Satan's ensnarement of Eve?

THE ENMITY OF THE WOMAN

4. "I will put enmity between you and the woman" (Genesis 3:15). Review the definition of "enmity" and the accompanying comments on page 128. What is God actually saying to Satan concerning the woman?

A Closer Look at God's Truth

THE SEED OF THE WOMAN

5. What happened when Adam "'transferred his allegiance from God to Satan'" (p. 129) and what was the result?

6. God would not leave the earth and humanity in their fallen condition forever. What does the second part of Genesis 3:15 tell us about God's way of recovery?

7. "Heaven and earth's greatest victory would be realized out of the greatest point of defeat" (p. 129). Describe how this statement applies to Eve as representative of woman in God's design.

THE AUTHORITY RETURNED
"When Jesus, the perfect Seed, came forth through woman, and the Seed went down into death, it looked as though Satan had won again" (p. 129), yet this act was the very crushing of Satan's head and the death blow to his authority. As God, the Son, Jesus was always in authority over Satan; this is not something He had to do for Himself.

8. On whose behalf was Jesus acting and why?

   Describe what part humanity now plays in response to Jesus' work for them and why.

THE STRENGTH OF AN ARMY

9. God has uniquely designed woman to enter into His work of recovery in the earth. Throughout the book of Proverbs the godly woman is called a "virtuous" (*chayil*) woman. What is the essence of this word and what does it tell us about the virtuous woman?

   Think of the people in your life. Who is someone you consider virtuous? Is being virtuous innate? Is it possible to *become* a virtuous person? How?

WARRING HANDS

10. Read Proverbs 14:1 as quoted on page 131. What does this verse tell us about the power of a woman's hands?

11. Two kinds of hands are mentioned in Proverbs 31, both of which are used to build her house. Describe the meaning of both kinds of hands. Also note the meaning of "fingers."

12. A virtuous woman is one "whose heart is turned to God, she has begun to see things from His perspective, from His eternal outlook" (p. 131). Read DeVern Fromke's statement beginning at the bottom of page 131. How does this statement relate to the virtuous woman?

13. The wilderness wandering of the Israelites was symbolic of a people delivered from Satan (Pharaoh) and the world (Egypt) but still dependent on their self-life. When Israel prepared to leave the wilderness behind and cross Jordan to possess the land that God had promised them, what was the response of the Canaanites and how does this principle apply to the Christian?

SHE SHALL REJOICE IN TIME TO COME

14. "'Rejoice' means 'to laugh or hold in derision, contempt or scorn.' It also means to 'mock or ridicule'" (p. 133). Who is it the woman will hold in contempt or scorn?

When Eve chose to make the breach between herself and Satan by exposing him as the deceiver, what did God do?

How does Satan come against woman and why?

EYES TO SEE

"Satan's tactics will work only as long as the woman herself is blind to her role and to the power God has given her to fulfill it" (p. 134).

15. Explain what happens when a woman becomes "virtuous," i.e., awakened to her womanhood as God purposed it from the beginning.

"The fear of the LORD is the beginning of wisdom" (Proverbs 9:10). The Lord wants us to be wise.

16. Read Ephesians 1:17-23. What does verse 17 tells us is the way we receive the spirit of wisdom and revelation?

Verses 18-23 are the revelation knowledge of Jesus Christ that Paul wanted us to have in order to return us to God's original intention for us. Explain this revelation and why it is essential for us to have it (see the last paragraph of page 134 continuing on to page 135).

17. Read Ephesians 2:5,6 which declares that we, too, were raised up with Christ by the same power that raised Him and were seated with Him in the same heavenly places. Why is it critical for us to know this and how does it affect our authority in the spiritual realm?

Explain how such knowledge affects the virtuous woman and how it relates to the work of her hands.

THE TRAVAILING WOMAN

18. Explain how woman is innately designed to participate in the bringing forth of life in the spiritual realm.

SPIRITUAL REPRODUCTION

"Prayer is not something we do to try to force God's hand, to try to convince Him to do something He does not want to do" (p. 137).

19. Review and explain the circle of prayer as described on page 136.

20. Read Matthew 6:9,10. What has always been God's intent for prayer?

Prayer is implementing God's decisions. It is enforcing God's will on earth. On pages 137-139 Jane describes her own awakening as she came into the knowledge of what it means to be a "virtuous woman." She began to understand God's will for herself, for her family and the part she was to play in it. Knowing His will, she began to enter in to bring it to pass.

21. Read Proverbs 31:22 which describes the clothing of the virtuous woman. Explain what it means to be clothed in "fine linen and purple" (beginning at the bottom of page 137 and on to page 138).

22. Read John 14:13,14; 15:7,8,16 as quoted on page 138. Why does God want to answer our prayers?

THE FRUIT OF HER SEED
Often in the Bible there is a physical reality that is also symbolic of a spiritual truth. Genesis 3:16, spoken to the woman, is one such example: "I will greatly multiply your sorrow and your conception; in pain you shall bring forth children."

23. Describe the spiritual principal that is being symbolized here (see pp. 139-140).

GIVE HER THE FRUIT OF HER HANDS
"The virtuous woman is a warrior woman. She allows God to teach her hands to war and her fingers to fight. She takes her stand against God's enemy, Satan, and refuses to back down until she sees total victory" (p. 140).

24. Read the story of the persistent widow in Luke 18:1-8 and the short two-paragraph paraphrase beginning at the bottom of page 140. How does this parable relate to the virtuous woman?

25. Proverbs 31:31 is the final pronouncement upon the virtuous woman. What are we told is her reward?

A Closer Look at My Own Heart

Although our attention has been specifically focused on women in this chapter, both men and women were described by the Hebrew word *chayil* in the Old Testament. When used in reference to men, they were described as warriors. When *chayil* referred to women it was translated "virtuous." Men and women alike are called to this kind of birthing, warring, interceding prayer that will bring forth life in the kingdom of God. This is not a burden; it is a great privilege and promise of reward that we have been given by God.

26. Think about what has been your heart perception of prayer. Has it been that of a beggar—one who approaches a reluctant God, but by appealing to His mercy you hope to get at least a few crumbs, or by some chance miracle you might hit on the right formula and one of your pleas might get a response? Perhaps you have thought prayer is about getting God to agree with you about what is needed in a given situation. In other words, that prayer is only about you, i.e., your will, your goodness, your worthiness to ask.

    Discuss and/or write down some of your thoughts.

27. Write down or discuss how this chapter has affected your understanding of prayer.

Action Steps I Can Take Today

As a Christian abiding in Christ you can begin to count on the fact that if something concerns you it does so because it concerns God. He very likely has planted it in your heart and is stirring you to action—prayer.

28. Take the concerns of your heart to God with a new confidence, knowing that He has called you for this very purpose. He wants to glorify and manifest Himself through His answers to your prayers. He wants to bring His kingdom to the earth through you.

29. Write down and meditate on John 15:7,8 as your confidence this week.

Eleven

A GOD OF PURPOSE

I know that You can do everything, and that no purpose of
Yours can be withheld from You. Job 42:2

God is a God of purpose. From Genesis to Revelation God has had one thing
in mind: to gain a family, a people for Himself who would intimately know
Him and out of that personal knowledge express His image and nature in the
earth through His own life and power. Everything from beginning to end God
has caused to work "after the counsel of His will...that we...should be to the
praise of His glory" (Ephesians 1:11,12, *NASB*).

The journey to accomplish this has been a lengthy one (at least from our
human viewpoint), and the Bible is replete with story after story weaving
together many events that tell us how God has gone about the process of
fulfillment. Men and women alike were used at critical junctures in history that
forever affected the outcome of God's plan.

Most of us assume that God can and will use men as He works out His will in the earth. When we think of Bible heroes, people like Joseph, David, Gideon, Samson and Daniel quickly spring to mind. Less instinctively we are reminded of the great women in the Bible. If we are to be reconciled, male and female, we must have a new understanding of the value of each. Our goal in this chapter is to determine that indeed God is always working everything together for His distinct purpose and also to affirm how specifically and strategically He has used women down through history in the furtherance of that purpose.

A Closer Look at the Problem

The story of Job vividly demonstrates the truth of our first goal. Job had known about God; he had even known how God wanted him to behave—righteously—and he was diligent to be obedient. He was a generous man who gave to the poor and shunned evil. Like the apostle Paul, Job was "blameless" concerning the law—he was righteous in his behavior. Both Job and his "friends" thought that Job's behavior was the most important thing to God. Whether or not Job had sinned and thereby deserved his trials was the substance of their arguments.

Job's friends were convinced he had sinned, but he consistently responded with protestations of good works and innocence of evil throughout the book.

1. Read Job 13:3,15,16 in *NASB* or translations other than *KJV* and *NKJV*. Even though Job asserts that his hope is in God, what do his words tell us he is depending on to justify himself before God?

The essence of Job's argument was "If I could just get an audience with God, I would tell Him how good I've been and He would lift this trial from me" (author's paraphrase). "My ways...will be my salvation," Job proclaims (vv. 15,16, *NASB*). Even though he declared he trusted God, his words reveal he believed his own good behavior would commend him to God's grace.

After a lengthy, distressing and painful testing of his faith, however, Job came to a new understanding of God. In spite of all his own confusion, in spite of all the accusations and continual haranguing of his so-called comforters, God's purpose in allowing the trial was fulfilled.

A Closer Look at God's Truth

2. Read Job 42:5 as quoted on page 143. When Job said "now my eye sees You," what was he really saying?

    Certainly our behavior is important to God, but what is most important to Him?

    What was God's ultimate purpose in Job's life?

A NEW VIEWPOINT

3. Because of Job's trial he began to see things from God's perspective. There was "a vital turning of his center and a personal revelation" (p. 144). What was Job's personal revelation?

4. Because of his trial, Job also gained a new and profound confidence in God. Read Job 42:2, *AMP*, as quoted at the end of the first paragraph on page 144. What was the confidence Job expressed?

    What is one of the key elements of purpose and why is this so?

PEOPLE OF PURPOSE

God is a God of purpose and we are a people of purpose. "No one or nothing [can] hinder that purpose from coming forth! Not our confusion, not our ignorance, not even our seeming inability for a time to cooperate with [God] will derail His plan. God is greater than all of it!" (p. 145).

5. Explain how this fact is played out in our daily lives and what God's purposed end result always is (see pp. 144-145).

God has always worked purposefully in the lives of His people, though sometimes He works so naturally through us that at the time we are not aware something divine is happening. Let's look at how this was often the case as God moved through women throughout history for the furtherance of His plan on earth.

The Divine Destiny of a Nation

6. Read the quotes concerning women beginning at the bottom of page 145 and following. Do you agree with these comments? Why?

These are the comments of people in our day, but this is not a new viewpoint. Think back in Bible history. Moses was perhaps the most illustrious deliverer of all time in the minds of the Jewish people. Yet he did not arrive on the scene of Israel's cruel time of slavery and bondage by himself. Three women played key roles in Moses' life.

7. Who were these women and how were they related to Moses?

What kind of a woman was God looking for as a mother for this great deliverer He was about to bring to the Jewish people (see p. 147)?

Why would it have been so easy to miss Jochabed's influence and heroism in this drama?

The Fearless Faith of a Woman

"Hebrews 11:23…says it was 'by faith' Moses was hidden by his parents, 'because they saw he was a beautiful [special] child; and they were not afraid of the king's command'" (p. 147).

8. "Imagine the day Jochebed placed Moses in that basket among the reeds in the river, knowing the reality of the situation" (p. 147). What were some of the dangers Jochebed's baby most likely faced that day?

9. God Himself orchestrated the events, yet each woman who responded that day did so out of the naturalness of her heart as a woman. Describe each woman's response and how it related to her nature as a woman.

"The response of these three women resulted in God's plan moving one step forward. Because of the faith and trust of Jochebed and Miriam, and even the unwitting response of the heart of Pharaoh's daughter, God was able to use them in an ordinary, yet clear and strategic way."

God is able to overcome every obstacle in our lives. "He will make even idolaters and idolatrous situations serve to further His plan" (p. 148).

10. What does this story tell us about God's ability to fulfill His purpose in our own lives?

WHAT IS IN YOU?

This is the story of Hannah, a woman who had a fertility problem. "The Bible simply says of Hannah that 'the LORD had shut up her womb' (1 Samuel 1:5, KJV)" (p. 148).

11. What was Hannah's emotional state over her condition and how do you think the enemy took advantage of her vulnerable condition?

What can we learn from Hannah's story about the way Satan works in our lives?

"It is important for us to recognize that God was in the midst of Hannah's barrenness. He was again orchestrating something from heaven for the furtherance of His plan and purpose on earth" (p. 149).

12. Describe how Hannah's condition matched the condition of Israel at that time and how this story exemplifies the "circle of prayer" we mentioned in the previous chapter.

13. Read 1 Samuel 1:11. What does this verse imply happened to Hannah before God answered her prayer?

14. Hannah's petition was granted and "the purpose of God moved another step forward" (p. 150). What does Hannah's story teach us about the burdens in our own lives and the way God works?

What does God often want to do in us before He answers our petitions?

A Woman of Understanding
The first thing Scripture tells us about Abigail is that she was a "woman of good understanding" (1 Samuel 25:3). Abigail had a very difficult marriage. "She was married to a man named Nabal, an alcoholic. His name means 'fool'" (p. 151).

15. Describe what Nabal was like and what kind of life Abigail must have had with him.

16. "Abigail...learned some things out of her need, out of her furnace of affliction" (p. 153). What had Abigail allowed God to do in her life in the midst of her pain?

Enter Abigail
A potentially deadly situation had arisen in Nabal's and Abigail's lives. Nabal, in his typical arrogant way, would not respond to David's request for food for his men, even though they had protected Nabal's men and flocks from marauders in the fields. David was angry and threatened to obliterate every man under Nabal's authority. One of Nabal's servants beseeched Abigail to respond to the crisis.

17. How did Abigail respond and what was the heart attitude of her response (see p. 154.)?

"God sent Abigail to influence David at a critical juncture in his life. David's eternal throne and the ongoing purposes of God on earth were forever affected by her action. Through a woman, the plan of God had taken another step forward" (p. 155).

THROUGH WISDOM A HOUSE IS BUILT

18. Read Proverbs 24:3, *AMP*, as quoted beginning at the bottom of page 155 and following. How does Abigail's behavior give us a "picture of what God has in His heart for woman" (p. 155)?

19. Briefly describe how Sarah, and then Esther, affected the history of God's people by their wise words and behavior (see p. 156).

"All of these women, along with many others in Scripture, were 'life-givers' [the name given to Eve by Adam], both by their actions and by their words" (p. 156).

20. Even though God has indeed called upon women throughout the centuries to turn and preserve whole nations through their godly wisdom and courage for His own sake and purpose, how have women in general been perceived?

21. "Jesus came to change all that. He came to die for the sin of humanity—the sin that caused separation, hostility, guarded self-protectiveness—for a world in which the weak are vulnerable to the strong" (p. 156). Read Joel 2:28,29 and Galatians 3:28. What do these verses tell us is God's intent for the functioning of His "house," both our "individual" houses and the House of the Lord (p. 157)?

What is the strength of the Church and why?

A Closer Look at My Own Heart

A key element of purpose is the turning of our center so that we see life from God's perspective—in other words, what He wants to accomplish in and through His people for His own sake. One of His purposes is to restore the respect of male and female in His Church, to bring unity and thereby strengthen us for the work He has given us to do.

22. Examine your own heart before the Lord. Whether you are male or female, what has been your thinking regarding women in the family, the Church and the nation? Discuss this with your group and/or write down your answers.

In the next chapter we will turn the tables and ask the same question regarding men.

Action Steps I Can Take Today

23. Ask someone to pray with you regarding your response to question 22. If there are attitudes that need to be changed, ask God to give you a revelation by His Holy Spirit so that you are changed from within.

    If you have strong attitudes of respect and inclusion concerning the value of women, ask God to strengthen you even more and show you how to communicate those attitudes to the Church.

24. Write down and memorize Job 42:2 as your encouragement concerning this issue.

– Twelve –

THE HEARTS OF THE FATHERS

Behold, I will send you Elijah the prophet before the coming
of the great and dreadful day of the LORD. And he will turn
the hearts of the fathers to the children, and the hearts of the
children to their fathers, lest I come and strike
the earth with a curse. Malachi 4:5,6

In the previous chapter we stated, "If we are to be reconciled, male and female, we must have a new understanding of the value of each." Our focus was the affirmation of women as we studied how God, throughout the ages, has strategically and specifically worked through them at critical junctures in history for the furtherance of His purpose.

Our goal in this chapter is to affirm how men are equally and inextricably essential to God's unfolding plan, how their place has never been more vitally under attack than it is today and how the presence of women in a man's life helps equip him to fulfill his role in the family, the Church and society.

100

A Closer Look at the Problem

1. Read the quote by Dr. James Dobson on page 160. Where does Dr. Dobson say we are in history and what does our very survival depend upon?

FATHERHOOD—CENTER STAGE

The Old Testament closes and in the New Testament the book of Luke opens with the same important words: "He will also go before Him in the spirit and power of Elijah 'to turn the hearts of the fathers to the children'" (Luke 1:17). Although John the Baptist began this work, there is a twofold fulfillment. Malachi declares this will take place before "the great and dreadful day of the LORD," which speaks of the day of God's wrath poured out on the unbelieving world.

2. Read the account in Luke 1:17. What does this verse tell us is the purpose for this turning?

"Fatherhood is suffering great fragmentation in today's world" (p. 161).

3. Read David Blankenhorn's statement from his book *Fatherless America*. What do you think about Blankenhorn's comment?

THE EROSION OF MORAL AND ETHICAL IDEALS

"The cost of fatherlessness to us as a society has been so immense that it defies adequate description. No part of our lives has remained unaffected" (p. 161).

4. Read the quotes and accompanying comments by William Bennett and Aleksandr Solzhenitsyn beginning at the bottom of page 161 and following. What is the cause of the erosion and decay in our society?

THE ENEMY COMES IN LIKE A FLOOD

"How did we get to where we are today? Has God been caught off guard, or has He been fully aware and fully active in the very center of the destruction? Let's trace the events of the past 40 years and see" (p. 162).

5. Explain what began to happen in the 1950s in the university campuses across the United States and what message was being trumpeted.

"Scripture and history are replete with evidence that nations rise or fall depending on their moral behavior" (p. 162).

6. On what had America been built and what were the effects of the words of the radicals and free thinkers?

7. During this same time frame "God began to raise up another voice on earth" (p. 162). Who was this person and what was his message?

8. "With advent of television in the mid-1950s, the media was now able to enter not only homes, but also the minds of the public" (p. 163). How was all of society ultimately affected as they unwittingly allowed themselves to become receptacles of the liberal and ungodly rhetoric of the media?

How has the Church been affected by this invasion?

9. "Coming alongside, however, and happening in concert with this moral revolution, was another revolution" (p. 163). What was this revolution and what was God doing?

RADICAL SECULAR FEMINISM

10. "At the dawning of the 1970s, the sexual revolution was in full swing. With it came another expression of dissidence, another voice containing another message escalating in intensity" (p. 163). What was this voice and what was the message?

Explain the cause of this uprising.

Although there were legitimate inequalities that needed to be addressed, time and investigation have revealed that the feminist agenda contained "virulent hidden factors and motives that strike at the very heart and harmony of family life as it has been defined in the past" (p. 164).

11. Read the statement by Robert Bork on page 164. Explain what he says radical feminism is and what it proposes to accomplish.

12. "Feminism strikes at the foundation of society. Indeed, it attacks the very heart of God's plan for man and woman and, ultimately, the Church" (p. 164). What is one of the goals of radical feminists as it relates to men (see the bottom of page 164 continuing to page 165)?

13. "In the midst of all this, there is not only a dismantling of femininity, but also of gender itself....Such artificial separating of the sexes to live independently of one another strikes right at the core and heart of God's plan" (p. 165). How is this so and what can we conclude about the source of this agenda?

THE FLIGHT OF FATHERS

14. "The flight of fathers from the home has come hard on the heels of the feminist agenda" (p. 165). What things have worked together to cause the flight of fathers from the home?

15. "What is the answer to the ever-widening disparity between men and women and the resultant destructive, moral and spiritual problems that are tearing at the fabric of society? Is it social reform?" (p. 166). Read Isaiah 60:2,3 as quoted on page 166 and the accompanying comments. Explain in your own words how God intends the Church to make a difference in today's fragmented society.

THE FATHER HEART OF GOD

One of the themes in this book is that God is first of all a Father.

> Everything He is, everything He says, everything He does, flows out of His Father heart. He longs to share Himself, to demonstrate and express His Father heart—His heart of tender mercy and compassion, along with His strength and leadership....
>
> Jesus repeatedly said He had come to "show us the Father," that in knowing Him, we would become like Him (see 2 Corinthians 3:18). Earthly fathers were to express their heavenly Father to their families. Sadly, this has not always been the case (p. 167).

16. Why have earthly fathers not always been able to love well?

A Closer Look at God's Truth

THE HELPER

17. At the height of the radical feminist movement God was bringing forth a women's movement of His own. What was this movement and what was its emphasis?

18. Although this movement started well, it "got sidetracked into a legalism that, for a time, sabotaged what God had begun" (p. 168). Explain the essence of this teaching and how it militated against God's design for woman.

19. Even though the Renewal Movement floundered, "God was not caught off guard. Time was not wasted as [God] continued to work" (p. 168). What has God been doing in this intervening 30 years in the lives of women?

MARRIAGE BY DESIGN

There has been great purpose in what God has been doing in the lives of women. "Let's revisit the design of woman for a moment because this truth is critical to the welfare of the family, the Church and the nation, and it will help us understand one of the significant ways God will 'turn the hearts of the fathers' in this precarious hour" (p. 169).

"Marriage, although intended to be the source of great blessing and satisfaction, was, from the beginning, also remedial. It was the 'remedy' to a problem—the man's aloneness. His condition was 'not good.' God observed that he would be greatly helped by a wife" (p. 169).

20. Read the quote from James Dobson in reference to *Men and Marriage*, a book by George Guilder. Explain in your own words the effect marriage (and a wife) has on the natural drives of men.

21. All of this doesn't happen automatically, however. We must walk with purpose according to God's design. Woman was designed to help resolve the aloneness of the man so that he is more equipped to function in his place in the family, Church and society. Describe how the woman is designed and how her design brings help to the problem (see p. 170).

22. The success of God's design will depend on the receptivity of the man. What is it that is essential for the man to understand about the woman's need for relationship?

23. Explain one of the primary purposes of God in the arena of marriage (see p. 171).

24. "As the husband is beckoned out of his aloneness, his heart becomes enlarged to truly know his wife, to live with her according to understanding. With this communion comes a greater knowing on at least four additional levels" (p. 171). Read the statements by John Powell and Paul Tournier on page 171. How do their comments apply to this first additional level of knowing?

25. Describe the other three levels of knowing and how the woman is instrumental in these interactions.

"It is interesting that, although Adam was eventually to have dominion over the earth, he was first instructed to 'keep' (guard and protect) the garden, his home, the place where he lived. Because he did not do so, the enemy entered. Adam lost not only the garden, but the earth as well....Eve, through ignorance, failed to be the help the man needed" (p. 172).

26. What has been the result of Adam's and Eve's failures?

What will be the answer to this devastation?

A Closer Look at My Own Heart

Families today, within and without the Church, are suffering immensely from the loss of fathers. In the worst case scenarios fathers are gone altogether. In some cases fathers are physically present in the home but relationally absent.

For whatever reason, men are suffering great disrespect in the eyes of many women and their value in the home is seen to be expendable at best or part of the problem at worst. Men themselves are often not cognizant of the great need of their involvement in the home and see themselves as unnecessary on many fronts.

27. Examine your own heart before the Lord. Whether you are male or female, what has been your thinking regarding men in the family, the Church and the nation?

Discuss this with your group or write down your answers.

Action Steps I Can Take Today

28. Ask someone to pray with you regarding your response to question 27. If there are attitudes that need to be changed, ask God to give you a revelation by His Holy Spirit so that you are changed from within.

    If you have strong attitudes of respect and inclusion concerning the value of men, ask God to strengthen you even more and show you how to communicate those attitudes to the Church.

Thirteen

WILL NOT GO WITHOUT YOU

And Barak said to her, "If you will go with me, then I will go; but if you will not go with me, I will not go!" Judges 4:8

Reconciling Men and Women to God's Original Design is the subtitle of our book and such has been the focus of our study. We began at the beginning, looking at the Father heart of God desiring a family in which He would dwell by His Spirit and thereby reproduce Himself. His offspring would be in His image which He declared would be fundamentally manifest in male and female.

Satan, knowing that in order for God's image to be expressed in the earth, male and female would have to function together, immediately attacked God's plan at the core. By leading the man and woman away from God's life and turning them to their own self-centers (as symbolized in the tree of the knowledge of good and evil), he brought separation, alienation, hostility and hiddenness to that first couple. That separation is not limited to husbands and wives, but it affects all relationships everywhere. The Church itself is not yet fully recovered from Satan's great coup and our goal in this study has not only been to discover God's original design, but also to uncover the many ways our self-centers are manifested, the ways they hinder us from the reconciliation and intimacy that would fulfill God's plan for us.

Our goal in this, our concluding chapter, is twofold. It is to again emphasize and affirm that God indeed has an original design, and also that He has been specifically moving in unprecedented ways in these important days, restoring His house, His family, the Church, to His design that "He might come...and fill [us] with His glory" (p. 14).

We will dispense with the category, A CLOSER LOOK AT THE PROBLEM, and devote our full attention in this final chapter to God's solution to our need.

A Closer Look at God's Truth

The story of Deborah in the book of Judges profoundly exemplifies the truth of our intended goals in this chapter. As Deborah appears in the annals of Scripture, God's people were again doing "evil in the sight of the LORD" (Judges 4:1). The cause of their evil behavior is summed up in Judges 21:25: "In those days there was no king in Israel; everyone did what was right in his own eyes." As a result the Lord had sold them into the hand of their enemy, King Jabin, the Canaanite. For 20 years they suffered great oppression "until in their desperation they cried out to the Lord for help. And God sent help—by way of a woman. Her name was Deborah" (p. 175).

1. Name the several roles that Deborah filled.

   What were the responsibilities of one who was a judge and also a prophet?

2. Explain the meaning and root meanings of Deborah's name and how this meaning fits in with the design of woman as discussed in previous chapters.

3. "Because of her intimate relationship with God, [Deborah] was also a warrior, a military leader who moved with great wisdom and authority."

When "she had heard by the Spirit that it was time to end the oppression of King Jabin....she summoned Barak" (p. 176). Who was Barak and what kind of a man was he?

What was Barak's response to Deborah and what do you think his motivation was?

What was most important to Barak?

Describe the result in the battle they fought together.

What qualified each of them for leadership? (Explore this further—what does this say to you?)

ON SONS AND DAUGHTERS

4. Read Joel 2:28,29. Explain the significance of this prophecy as it related to each class of people.

What was the most radical part of this prophecy and why is this so?

How does this prophecy relate to the restoring and reconciliation of God's house?

"God...*is* moving us forward into a new day. He is revealing His heart for His people. He is moving to reconcile us, not only as a corporate Church and as couples, but also as individuals. He is reconciling us to ourselves at the core of our beings. Before women could fully move into their designed place, much healing had to occur. Years of demoralizing hurt, discrimination and disrespect needed to be healed." Let's look for a moment at one person in Scripture who "vividly exemplifies the condition of women down through the centuries...the bent-over woman of Luke 13" (p. 179).

A WOMAN SET FREE FROM BONDAGE

5. Review the story of the bent-over woman (beginning on page 179 and following). Describe this woman's condition and how it would have affected her functioning.

Who are we told is responsible for her crippled condition?

6. Jesus came to earth to "destroy the works of the devil" (1 John 3:8). What were His words to this woman and what was the effect on her? Elaborate.

7. Who was the most indignant about the woman's healing, and what reason did Jesus give for His actions?

A NEW QUESTION

8. How might this story relate to what God has been doing in the lives of women in the past 30 years?

THE HEART OF THE ISSUE

9. "Such is the purpose behind this deep work of healing God has been doing in the heart of woman. Incapable of raising herself, God, by His Spirit, has been awakening and reconciling her to her womanhood as He meant it to be" (p. 182). Why is it imperative that this reconciliation occur within a woman's own heart and spirit first?

10. "The restoration God desires for women is not about positions on church boards...whether they can be pastors or leaders and still be 'doctrinally correct'" (p. 182). What is the real issue and why is it so important?

CALL FOR THE MOURNING WOMEN

11. Read Jeremiah 9:17-21 as quoted beginning on page 183. How would you relate this passage to life as it is today?

Again in our day, God has "been calling for the mourning, praying women....For many women, the great substance of their prayers has been for their husbands, the fathers of their children. Today we are seeing vast evidence that God has begun to move and answer those prayers in a mighty way" (p. 184).

AN UNPRECEDENTED MOVE AMONG MEN

12. Review Jeremiah 9:19 and the comments from the *Bethany Parallel Commentary* as quoted under this subheading in the book. Explain what is really happening in this verse.

13. Read the statement by Randy Phillips as quoted on page 185. What incredible evidence do we have that women's prayers have been heard and that truly a response is "coming out of Zion" (p. 184)?

In response to what we see happening among men, Ken R. Canfield says, "It's as if our male culture were collectively looking at their watches and saying, 'It is five o'clock, time to go home'" (p. 185).

14. Read Malachi 4:5,6. How does this present move among men relate to the fulfillment of this prophecy?

WHY SUCH A MOVE AMONG MEN?

15. Read the statement made by Dave McCoombs beginning at the bottom of page 185. To what does he attribute this move among men?

    Describe the events that precipitated this crisis in masculinity. Are there other factors that you would add?

16. What would be some of the enemy's goals in causing an angry, militant uprising among women?

DON'T MISS WHAT GOD IS DOING

Previously we mentioned that God was reconciling women to the core of their own being, to their womanhood as God meant it to be.

17. Read the rest of Dave McCoombs's statement beginning at the bottom of page 186. Describe what we see happening in this men's movement.

    Do you think all of this is just coincidence or do you think God is doing something? If so, what?

    What must be the response of women to this amazing work of God?

WHERE THE LORD COMMANDS THE BLESSING

18. What is the "bottom line of everything Jesus came to do" (p. 187)? Elaborate.

19. "When our relationships are right, when we are walking in true intimacy with God and others" (p. 188), what will happen in the lives of those who are truly seeking the meaning of life?

Why? What do you think the world is really searching for?

The immense mandate of purpose God has for His Church cannot be the result of our own self-effort. We need His anointing, His life, His blessing.

20. Read Psalm 133 as quoted on page 188. What are we told brings the anointing, the life and the blessing of God?

What can we conclude will be the state of the Church if we do not respond to this call of God's Spirit for unity at every level?

21. How can we apply Barak's statement, "I will not go without you" (Judges 4:8) to our lesson today?

God has a purpose and a design for His family, the Church, through which He desires to fill everything everywhere with Himself. His purpose (and the explanation of His design) is that first and most important, we would know Him. We have been "fashioned for intimacy," for relationship, first of all with God. Secondly and consequently, our purpose is that we would express His character, nature, authority and power on the earth.

His design is that we be like Him, restored to His image through the working of His own Spirit within us. Inextricable to this design and foundational to everything God wants to do, is that we become one. Only together are we His complete image, "the church,...the fullness of Him who fills all in all" (Ephesians 1:22,23). Together we are "Christ," the "one new man" through whom God always intended to express Himself in the earth (see 1 Corinthians 12:12, Ephesians 2:15).

In this study guide we have been faced with the truth that all God wants to do in and through our lives is contingent upon the way we relate to the rest of His body of which male and female are the smallest microcosm. We have been fashioned for intimacy, not only with God but with each other. Our restored relationships are the foundation of the restored power of God to the Church.

A Closer Look at My Own Heart

Unity in the Church worldwide must begin in the heart of each person in the sphere of his or her own environment. We must begin with ourselves.

22. As we conclude this study, ask the Holy Spirit to search your heart. Are there any judgments or strongholds in your life that would be a hindrance to complete reconciliation or the restoration of true relationship with any segment of the Body of Christ?

   Consider your attitudes toward yourself, those of other denominations, races, cultures and particularly those of the opposite gender. Is there any part of Christ's Body—the Church—that you have seen as less valuable than other parts, or do you see all as equally and vitally necessary to the fulfillment of God's plan for His people?

Discuss this with your group and/or write down your answers.

Action Steps I Can Take Today

23. If God shows you places of prejudice that are keeping you alienated from other people—even if it is a private, inner alienation—share your insight with at least one other person and ask him or her to pray with you for repentance and a restored attitude.

24. Pray for each other that your understanding of God's design for you will enlarge and that He will continue to heal you of any hindrances that will prevent you from entering into His full inheritance.

25. Commit to memory the essence of Barak's short but profound statement as a reminder of God's design for His Body, but particularly as it relates to male and female as the indivisible foundation: "I will not go without you!"

What Is Aglow International?

From one nation to 135 worldwide...
From one fellowship to over 3,300...
From 100 women to more than 2 million...

Aglow International has experienced phenomenal growth since
its inception 30 years ago. In 1967, four women from the state
of Washington prayed for a way to reach out to other Christian
women in simple fellowship, free from denominational boundaries.

The first meeting held in Seattle, Washington, USA, drew more
than 100 women to a local hotel. From that modest beginning,
Aglow International has become one of the largest intercultural,
interdenominational women's organizations in the world.

Each month, Aglow touches the lives of an estimated two million women on six continents through local fellowship meet-
ings, Bible studies, support groups, retreats, conferences and various outreaches. From the inner city to the upper echelons, from
the woman next door to the corporate executive, Aglow seeks to
minister to the felt needs of women around the world.

Christian women find Aglow a "safe place" to grow spiritually
and begin to discover and use the gifts, talents and abilities God
has given them. Aglow offers excellent leadership training and
varied opportunities to develop those leadership skills.

Undergirding the evangelistic thrust of the ministry is an emphasis on prayer, which has led to an active prayer network linking
six continents. The vast prayer power available through Aglow
women around the world is being used by God to influence
countless lives in families, communities, cities and nations.

Aglow's Mission Statement

Our mission is to lead women to Jesus Christ and provide opportunity for Christian women to grow in their faith and minister to others.

—◦◦◦—

Aglow's Continuing Focus...

- To reconcile woman to her womanhood as God designed. To strengthen and empower her to fulfill the unfolding plan of God as He brings restoration to the male/female relationship, which is the foundation of the home, the church and the community.
- To love women of all cultures with a special focus on Muslim women.
- To reach out to every strata of society, from inner cities to isolated outposts to our own neighborhoods, with very practical and tangible expressions of the love of Jesus.

—◦◦◦—

Gospel Light and Aglow International present an important new series of Bible studies for use in small groups. The first two studies in the Aglow Bible Study Series, **Shame: Thief of Intimacy** *and* **Keys to Contentment***, are available through Gospel Light. Look for these and others in the Aglow Bible Study Series including Choosing to Change, Building Better Relationships and God's Character. For information about these and other outstanding Bible study resources from Aglow, call us at 1-800-793-8126.*

Aglow Ministers In...

Albania, Angola, Anguilla, Antigua, Argentina, Aruba, Australia, Austria, Bahamas, Barbados, Belgium, Belize, Benin, Bermuda, Bolivia, Botswana, Brazil, British Virgin Islands, Bulgaria, Burkina Faso, Cameroon, Canada, Cayman Islands, Chile, China, Colombia, Congo (Rep. of), Congo (Dem. Rep. of), Costa Rica, Côte d'Ivoire, Cuba, Curaçao, Czech Republic, Denmark, Djibouti, Dominica, Dominican Republic, Ecuador, Egypt, El Salvador, England, Equatorial Guinea, Estonia, Ethiopia, Faroe Islands, Fiji, Finland, France, Gabon, the Gambia, Germany, Ghana, Greece, Grenada, Guam, Guatemala, Guinea, Guyana, Haiti, Honduras, Hungary, Iceland, India, Indonesia, Ireland, Israel, Jamaica, Japan, Kazakstan, Kenya, Korea, Kyrgyzstan, Latvia, Malawi, Malaysia, Mali, Mauritius, Mexico, Fed. States of Micronesia, Mongolia, Mozambique, Myanmar, Nepal, Netherlands, Papua New Guinea, New Zealand, Nicaragua, Niger, Nigeria, Norway, Oman, Pakistan, Panama, Peru, Philippines, Portugal, Puerto Rico, Romania, Russia, Rwanda, Samoa (American), Samoa (Western), Scotland, Senegal, Sierra Leone, Singapore, South Africa, Spain, Sri Lanka, St. Kitts, St. Lucia, St. Maartan, St. Vincent, Sudan, Suriname, Sweden, Switzerland, Tajikistan, Tanzania, Thailand, Togo, Tonga, Trinidad/ Tobago, Turks & Caicos Islands, Uganda, Ukraine, United States, U.S. Virgin Islands, Uruguay, Uzbekistan, Venezuela, Vietnam, Wales, Yugoslavia, Zambia, Zimbabwe, plus one extremely restricted 10/40 Window nation.

How do I find my nearest Aglow Fellowship? Call or write us at:

AGLOW®
INTERNATIONAL

P.O. Box 1749, Edmonds, WA 98020-1749
Phone: (425) 775-7282 or 1-800-755-2456
Fax: (425) 778-9615   E-mail: aglow@aglow.org
Web site: http://www.aglow.org/

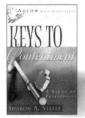

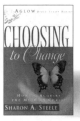

Let Jane Hansen Lead Your Next Study

Jane Hansen describes the true biblical relationship God yearns to have with each of us. Discover God's original plan for intimacy, and how men and women can be reconciled to Him and each other.

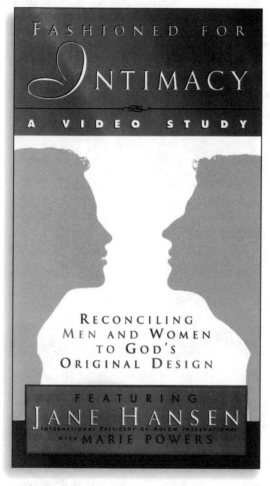

Video Study • UPC 607135.003649

Available at your local Christian bookstore.

Gospel Light